MW01620436

BLACK ANGELS

The Wealth Edition

Dr. Shanté P. Williams

Disclaimer

This Content is for informational purposes only, you should not construe any such information or other material as legal, tax, investment, financial, or other advice. Nothing contained in this book constitutes a solicitation, recommendation, endorsement, or offer by Dr. Shante Williams to buy or sell any securities or other financial instruments.

All Content on this book is information of a general nature and does not address the circumstances of any particular individual or entity. Nothing in this book constitutes professional and/or financial advice, nor does any information in this book constitutes a comprehensive or complete statement of the matters discussed or the law relating thereto. You alone assume the sole responsibility of evaluating the merits and risks associated with the use of any information or other Content in this book. Consult the approriate legal, tax, accounting, or financial professional

DEDICATION

This book is dedicated to all the capital activists that are moving money aroung the world. We will change the world, we will redefine success, we will get the capital into the hands of those who need it, and who can do the most good!

"Hope -- Hope in the face of difficulty. Hope in the face of uncertainty. The audacity of hope! In the end, that is God's greatest gift to us...A belief in things not seen. A belief that there are better days ahead."

— BARACK OBAMA

INTRODUCTION

Building generational wealth is a topic that makes an appearance with growing regularity. Generational wealth also referred to as "old money," means that the assets built in your lifetime are passed down to your children, grandchildren, and children after them. Before we begin to think about creating generational wealth, we must first build the current assets of the present generation.

In 2019, there were just under 10 million people with a net worth between $1 million and $5 million. Just under 2 million people have a net worth between $5 million and $25 million. It is not surprising that there are only 156,000 households with a net worth of $25 million or more. There are approximately 11.8 million millionaires in America, making up roughly 3.5% of the population. This would suggest that at least some have figured out how to build within the current system. Only 8% of those individuals with a net worth of $1 Million or more are Black. When considering all the factors that contribute to wealth there is approximately a 6.4% chance of becoming a millionaire if you are black.

It is no surprise that data from the 2019 Survey of Consumer Finances (SCF) show that wealth disparities between families in different racial and ethnic groups are nearly the same as the previous survey in 2016; The average White family has eight times the wealth of the average Black family and five times the wealth of the typical Hispanic family.

In the United States the pathways to creating wealth are well defined. Contrary to some previous generation understandings of getting ahead simply being the hardest worker will not lead you to financial stability and economic independence.

Let's start with some definitions. Wealth is defined as the difference between families' gross assets and their liabilities. The assets are the things that you own that hold and increase in value. The liabilities are the things that you owe on or that cost you money. For example, if you purchase a home that is worth $1 million dollars, and you own it with no mortgage then it is an asset that worth $1 million dollars. Adding the full value to your net worth. If that that same home that is has a $900,000 mortgage on it then the outstanding mortgage is a liability. So that same home only contributes $100,000 to your net worth.

Black Families Are Gaining Ground.

Between 2016 and 2019, median wealth went up for all races and ethnicity groups. Wealth for Black families grew at a rate of 33%. However, this growth rate did extraordinarily little to close the wealth gap. Black families are still re-gaining the ground lost from the great recession in 2008. There are still some misunderstandings about the things that really build wealth. Other than work as hard as possible, two additional paths have been pushed to African Americans if they want to build wealth: education and entrepreneurship. Education and entrepreneurship have become the perennial favorites proposed to help the community achieve economic success. However, while education and entrepreneurship are essential components of building wealth, they will not solely aid in building generational wealth.

Education has led to an increase in the professional class within the African American Community. According to the United States Census, since 1940, the percentage of Black Americans over the age of 25 who have attained a high school diploma has steadily increased from 7.7% in 1940 to 87.9% in 2018 (Bureau, 2019). The number of Black Americans over the age of 25 who have attained a bachelor's degree has also continued to rise from 1.3% in 1940 to 25.2% by 2018 (Bureau, 2019). However, these educational gains have barely made a dent in closing the wealth gap experienced in this country.

For Black Americans, entrepreneurship has long been a vehicle to gain a sense of independence and freedom by building their own enterprises. These businesses were at one time born out of necessity as there were few businesses that Blacks could patronize and be serviced appropriately. In fact, 1900-1930 is often referred to as the golden age of black entrepreneurship (Walker, 2009). By 2015, 2.6 million small businesses were owned by Blacks. However, only 4% of these businesses have paid employees, and access to capital is a significant impediment to high growth for many Black-owned small businesses irrespective of the industry.

This speaks to the need for African Americans to not only start businesses, but to also invest in them in order to help achieve new levels of success in the African American business community. A business that has the ability to grow and scale not only creates jobs but can create an asset that can last for generations.

By just focusing on those two pathways to wealth building, fundamental building blocks of wealth have traditionally been ignored.

Despite the glamorization of entrepreneurship, many have no desire or talent to build a company. But even though we may not all be able to be founders, we can all be OWNERS. Ownership is key. Ownership, whether it be real estate, or interest in stocks or companies, has helped create wealth that has been passed from one generation to another. Creating wealth is not merely the act of having an inheritance to give to your children-assets that continue to grow are critical. Once we become fully financially invested in industry and in our communities, then and only then can we say that we are fully invested in the future. Investors provide capital to businesses. For many of them, that capital is the difference between success and failure. As a result, investors chose winners and, by default, losers. Those that receive investments are more likely to thrive, and those that do not are more likely to operate in a survival mode that prevents real growth. According to the Angel Capital Association, only 1.3% of investors are Black. This lack of participation means that many people of color have never even met an active investor and do not know where to start.

Much has been touted about the need to create long-lasting wealth; however, very few books have shown people of color how to participate in the economy fully. In this book, we will discuss how to prepare your finances and lifestyle to become an investor, decide what to invest in, and how to earn investment income. As a Venture Capitalist and Angel Investor myself, I have deployed capital into many businesses.

My first investment was $1,000 into hair salon products. That investment was small in terms of dollars but outsized in terms of impact. That salon owner was able to put products on her shelves that helped to build a new stream of revenue. She was also able to reinvest the earnings and use it to drive further growth of her business. That business now has locations in 2 states, and continues to support a single mother, especially in helping her to pay for her child's college education.

As a Black Angel, I was able to help provide an opportunity for an entrepreneur who had been overlooked by other funders, and certainly not on the radar of traditional Angel Investors. We all are friends and family to someone, and this guide will prevent you from being a fool. I seek to equip a new Army of Black Angels that can move the needle for the Black Community and create lasting wealth that will mean real freedom for the next generation. I genuinely believe that everyone is capable of becoming an investor regardless of your income. The earliest investors in many start-ups and businesses are what I call the 3 F's: Friends, Family, and Fools. This becomw is intended to give you the information you need to become one of the few black angels that exist in the United States.

Before becoming Black Angels there needs to be a better understanding of wealth building basics. First, we will tackle the basics of wealth building: Income, Savings, Planning, Information, Credit, and Investment. It is important to have a good understanding of each of these pillars and incorporate them into your mindset and way of living. If we create holistic and realistic pathways toward economic mobility, we can defy the odds build wealth that can be transferred from generation to generation.

◆ ◆ ◆

It is time to watch our money grow, move, mature, and most importantly work for us.

PREFACE

Wealthy Roots

Communities around the world are beginning are awakening to the reality that if they want to achieve the financial stability and economic mobility, they must take their futures into their own hands. Governments and philanthropic organizations have shown us that NOBODY IS COMING TO SAVE US! Lower- and middle-income families must look inward. There are some lessons that must be unlearned. There is trauma that has to be recognized and there are new foundations that must be laid. To bear the fruit of wealth we must first address the roots. Make no mistake wealth is not simply a tabulation of how much money that is in your bank account, but it is a culmination of the behaviors, attitudes, and training that govern your life.

As I advise entrepreneurs and families on their wealth journey I am reminded of my own journey and the family roots that are beginning to bear fruit. My family is from Charlotte North Carolina, a city that was identified as a place where a child born into poverty has less than 5% chance of making it to the middle class. In short there are large swath of the city that may never even have a chance at achieving the "American Dream". I was one of the children able to live out that dream. In fact, my whole family was able to transcend poverty and defy the odds. By statistical probability we should all still live in public housing and be lucky to graduate from high school. However, we must remember that people are not statistics and truly anything is possible. When asked where we got our drive, I often say it was our wealthy roots that pushed us forward. No, we didn't have a rich uncle or a lottery winner but rather a mindset that meant that once we knew better, we did better. Here is our story.

I was born to two young parents. Both living in public housing but carrying a determination to graduate from high school and build. My mother recounts being 15 with a newborn and having to move in with my Father's family. There we lived in an apartment, with my aunt and cousins, everyone working to provide for their children and do better. Fast forward 38 years and everyone that lived in that tiny apartment now owns their own home, built careers, sent their kids to college, and have investment portfolios that will carry them through retirement and leave a legacy for their loved ones. THIS IS GENERATIONAL WEALTH.

So exactly what was being taught at 613 East 6th Street? The family mantra was simple:

- IF YOU WANT IT GO GET
- DON'T OWE NOBODY NOTHING
- WE ALL WE GOT
- ASK FOR HELP

There was no pretense about speaking well or keeping up appearances for the benefit of others. The three heads of household Sandra Diane Williams, Kenneth Williams, Vanessa Williams (now Vanessa Whitley) instilled these into all of the children and reinforced them by the way they lived.

IF YOU WANT IT GO GET IT

SANDRA WILLIAMS-HILL AKA AUNT DIANE

This seems like a simple lesson, but it is one that is often confused. Going for what you want was not just a simple act of toiling day after day but rather looking for examples and experiences that would help you achieve. The first task was getting out of that apartment and moving into a home. Not an easy feat in the late 80s. Diane, Ken, and Vanessa not only wanted to own homes, but they began to do the work to become the first generation of owners. They got educated on the housing market, what it took from an income and credit perspective, they learned the mortgage terms and secured home loans. Aunt Diane took charge of her life- she was often the person to take charge and get things done. She took care of her brothers and her family.

The wealth wisdom here is set a goal and then execute.

DON'T OWE NOBODY NOTHING

This is still one of my Father's favorite sayings. I can remember when he would say if I can not pay for it outright then I won't have it. The wealth wisdom in this is debt management. My father is fiscal conservative. He has always been vigilant about paying the bills and saving for the other things you wanted. This mindset demonstrated that acquiring things that you can not afford for the benefit of showing off will truly lead to a world of disappointment and discontent. Today, dad has been retirement eligible for years but works not because he has to but because he wants to. I attribute that level of comfort and stability to the fact that he owes 'NOBODY NOTHING'.

WE ALL WE GOT

Self-reliance is a wealth mindset that always pays dividends. It should not be confused with going alone but having the confidence in yourself and taking care of the things (and people) that matter. Vanessa Whitley has been a caregiver and provider from an early age. When her mother took ill and her father was killed when she was 9 years old, she famously pushed a chair up to the stove and tried to fry chicken to make a dinner for her younger sister. Today Vanessa aka Mom excels in her career, owns property, and has planned for the future by providing for her children and grandchildren. That forward planning is key to setting up the next generation. She took on estate planning as wealth wisdom because she knows other than God- WE ALL WE GOT.

ASK FOR HELP

To ask for help and not suffer in silence is a lesson that set up the next generation for wealth. My sisters, Tamara Williams and Jalisa Williams, and my nephew Kyrie Williams have used these keys to unlock and unveil a generation of owners. We from an early age were taught to not be ashamed to ask for help if we needed it and to find someone who knew more and learn from them. We have all applied these wealth keys. Creating generational wealth starts with a solid foundation. Its equipping yourself and your descendants to build, to own, to thrive in the face of adversity. To rage against the system not just in words but in actions. My wealthy roots have set me on a course to make impactful change and empower communities. They have helped to craft the fundamentals of wealth that I hope to pass on to as many people as possible.

PART I: BACK TO BASICS

Wealth Building Basics

In this first part we revisit what it known about building wealth. While the components are known, attaining them has increasingly become more difficult. Despite the increased focus on each of the individual factor individuals looking to make strides in closing the wealth gap must look to avenues that allow them to simultaneous improve their standing in each area.

As illustrated in the chart below Black wealth increases to just over $53,000 for adults over 55 years of age. While this is an improvement from the $600 for adults over 35 years of age it will hardly leave a legacy for the next generation.

	White	Black	Hispanic
Under 35	25.4	0.6	11.2
35-54	185.0	40.1	46.1
Over 55	315.0	53.8	111.5

Source: Federal Reserve Board, 2019 Survey of Consumer Finances

Notes: Table displays median wealth by age group and by race and ethnicity in thousands of 2019 dollars

The 4 basic building blocks of wealth are: Income, Savings, Ownership, and Planning. The value of each of these building blocks typically improves over time however for people of color the increase in wealth over one's age is simply not enough to increase the quality of life for the community. To accelerate the rise of wealth in the community we must take the building blocks and apply them to new fields like angel and venture investing to reclaim neighborhoods and build a more prosperous future.

CHAPTER ONE: CASH IN

Income

"A larger income is the best recipe for happiness."

\- Jane Austen

The journey to becoming an angel investor starts with the capital that you have coming in. The rules set forth by the Security and Exchange Commission concerning who can participate in certain types of deals is partially determined by the amount of income that you consistently make. In many instances people of color and women are in lower paying positions with limited ability for advancement. It is important to increase your income even if the gains are small. We will discuss the many ways to generate more income and aligning your mentality to making more money outside of your 9-5 job.

Income

Job vs Career

It does not take an economist or financial genius to point our that the money that you have coming in is a critical part of the wealth equation. For most people your nearly 100% of the money coming into your household is from your employer. If this is the case, then it is necessary to begin asking yourself several important questions. The first question you should be asking yourself is: *Is this a job or is this a career?* There are key differences in having a job versus having a career that have direct implications on building wealth.

A job is typically something that is done to simply earn a paycheck. A job is there to simply pay the bills. In general, you are not seeking advancement and may not intend to be in that position for the long-term. A career in the other hand is something that you intend to continue to move up and advance in. The difference between having a job and a career has a lot to do with your goals and your mentality not the industry or your current starting position.

If you find yourself with a job, then ask yourself whether you enjoy aspects of what you do. If you can find parts of that job that you like (other than the paycheck) make a list of those things and begin looking for a position that features the things you love. Converting your job to a career will mean that you will have the ability to bring in more income because you are able move up in the company or industry making more money. Let's take the classic example of a fast-food worker. This is typically looked at as a job and not a career, however there are people who have turned that job into a career. If you start as a Crew team member and making the federal minimum wage, working full-time, then before taxes you make $15,080 per year. This rate is just over the federal poverty line for a single person, likely not enough to live on without supplemental income assistance. If you were to move up to the next position of crew trainer, your income increases slightly to $15,080. While this will not lead to financial freedom it is a promotion that could be achieved in a few months, whether by moving up in your current restaurant or moving to another chain. The next promotion might be store manager. Yielding an increase to $16,287 annually, another small step. From there you might be able to move to area manager, a step that would increase your income $19,056. Continuing on this path in 2-3 three years of your restaurant career you may be able to move into corporate, increasing your salary to about $30-$40,000. The difference in those salaries is making a plan for advancement. Setting out goals and looking for how you might advance is key to continuing to bring in more income. The job market can be a very rough place if you do not have the benefit of education or experience but continue to seek opportunities within the company to learn a new skill that might help you move up. If you are in a career, changing positions can often be the way to increasing your income. Often times people in careers leave money on the table by not advocating for raises when your work performance is evaluated. Women are less likely to ask for a raise and that can lead to large pay differences over time. Be your own best advocate, you simply can rely on others seeing your value and equating that to dollars. Finally, know that your position is worth, both in your company and in your industry. Several online tools will equip you with insights into what other companies or sectors might pay for your skill set. Since we have already established that simply working harder will not make you wealthy there are other ways to directly increase the money into your bank account.

Calling All Side-Hustlers

A side hustle is not full-time business pursuit but rather something you do in your spare time to make extra money. This could mean participating in the gig economy and driving for a ride-share company or delivering food or groceries. It could also be converting a hobby into profit. If you properly control the expenses and other costs side hustling can add hundreds or thousands of dollars to your bank account. Even if you do not intend for your side hustle to be a business you must be sure to treat it like one. If you will be selling a good or service, then make sure you set your price to cover all your costs including your time. You should include taxes (which you do have to pay!) and shipping. You could also consider becoming an affiliate salesperson or ambassador for another business. This may reduce your upfront costs, but it will require diligent marketing and advertising which ultimately means your time.

Starting a Business

It is important to separate starting a full-time business from a side hustle. A business requires a different level of attention and commitment. As mentioned in the introduction entrepreneurship has been a consistent key to wealth building but only if that business is able to grow and scale. Taking the entrepreneurial leap requires preparation. If you begin a business before making a well thought out plan you could end up losing ground in your wealth building journey. Being an entrepreneur and running a business is nothing like the shiny stories we see on television or on social media. The process is often lonely, disappointing, filled with "learning opportunities" also known as failure and it may take three times longer for money to start coming in than you plan. If you are unsure whether you are ready for full-time entrepreneurship take the time to answer these questions.

Why am I starting this business?

Of course, the obvious answer is to make money but be specific. Do you want to create a business that supports your family, or do you want to create a business that will one day scale to a multi-million-dollar enterprise that ships all over the world? Do you want to sell the business off and live on those funds in retirement or do you want to pass the business on to your children? Why you're starting the business will directly shape how you build it.

Can I put in the necessary time to build?

A common misconception about entrepreneurship is that you

will be your own boss and you will have time to do all of the extra things you always wanted to. This likely will not be the case especially not early on. If you have other time obligations such as children, a spouse, or care giving for loved ones then you will need to create a life/work schedule that gives you time to build your business and take care of your family. Working from home and for yourself will require more discipline and intentionality. You will have to keep yourself on track and make time for self-care.

Do I have 12-18 months extra cash reserves?

This is generally the hardest question and for most people the answer is no. In years past the cash reserve was 6 months but after the great recession and a pandemic most experts suggest 12-18 months. We will speak on how to increase these savings in a later chapter. Do not make the mistake of thinking because you were at the top of your field that the sales will come pouring in. Your former employer may have a non-compete or a non-solicitation clause. You may have signed it in your initial human resources packet. These documents can prevent you from bringing certain clients into your new venture so make sure you double check that employee handbook.

Do I have a list of trusted professionals (lawyer, accountant, etc.) or do I need a referral?

A list of professionals is necessary. If you have no idea where to start you may want to visit your local government, chamber of commerce, or community college. They are great resources for business owners and can plug you into reputable professionals.

Can I take feedback? Lots and Lots of feedback... and not all of it constructive?

A famous entrepreneur was asked in a public forum: What words of encouragement can you offer entrepreneurs? His reply was if they need encouragement, they should do something else. It is not all negatives when you are building a business you will hear more no's than yes'. You will receive the opinions and "perspectives" from customers, banks, investors, and even strangers on social media. You have to be able to handle criticism and quickly develop a thick skin.

Who are my mentors and go-to people when I need help?

Similar to your trusted professionals you will need mentors and advisors who can help. Be sure to not just choose someone who claims to be a consultant. Check their references and make sure they have the relevant experience and background to be able to advise you properly.

How will my business make money? What is revenue generation strategy B-Z?

This seems like a no brainer—you will have customers who love your product and then they will tell their friends and they will buy and so on. You will have to decide who your customers are, Other businesses? Adults? Children? Will you sale online? Will you sell door to door? Will you use a subscription model?

Knowing how you will make money is one of the most complicated questions a business owner may have to answer.

What things do I LOVE handling? What things do you hate doing?

It will become important to identify your core talents and things you like handling and the things that you don't. Make no mistake you will likely have to do things that you hate but as you grow the company and look to grow you will need to fill in the gaps quickly to make generating money an easier process.

Who is doing the books and keeping finance in order?

Unless you are a certified professional account HIRE someone else to do the numbers or at least review them with you on a quarterly basis. This will help with tax preparation and building quality financial statements that will help you in the future.

Where is the start-up capital coming from? Will I be investing my own money?

This may be the most important question of all. Black businesses are generally undercapitalized. Often these businesses are utilizing the bootstrapping method well beyond the time when it is useful. If you still have a 9-5 think about securing capital before you lose your income. It may be helpful to get a line of credit or credit card that you reserve for use in case your business savings are depleted, and you aren't quite making money.

Chapter Summary/Key Takeaways

It is an easy thing to write that you should just make more money. The factors limiting your income generation may be extremely complicated. For many becoming a business owner or side hustler is the best avenue to making real gains. Regardless of where you are on the income scale it matters how you leverage the money that you have. Your mentality and attitude regarding your money play a direct role in how it might work for you. Create a plan. Even small increases can be valuable. In the next chapter we talk about building up your savings.

CHAPTER TWO: GETTING READY

"Save money and money will save you"

Jamaican Proverb

It is obvious that if you are going to build wealth you must hold on to at least some of your income after bills. Controlling your expenses can help to build wealth. Having savings can help deal with unexpected expenses. In the event that you do not have adequate savings to cover emergencies you may be forced into predatory lending practices like payday loans that can create serious long-term wealth killing repercussions. Building savings can be difficult at first however, you must really determine exactly what you have and where it all goes.

How to Determine How Much You REALLY Have

Personal Financial Audit

A personal financial audit can help decipher what your current financial status is. You'll be able to determine what your current net worth is, and most importantly, you'll be able to see areas where you can save costs so that you can afford to invest much quicker. Conducting a personal financial audit sounds more technical and more painful than it is. The best place to start is by looking at your current budget. Don't be embarrassed if you haven't been abiding by a budget. Start with the basics. How much money do you make per month? How much money do you spend?

A simple template is provided at the end of the chapter to help get you started. To get a proper gauge, use 3-6 months of bank statements because using just one month or two can give a false impression of your spending habits. Make notes of everything, no matter how small the purchase. Once you have a consistent number for what comes in and what goes out, start categorizing. The categories should be very descriptive; avoid, making broad bulk categories like miscellaneous or discretionary.

Once accurately categorized, separate all items into necessities/essentials and non-necessities.

The essentials are:

1. Shelter (rent/mortgage)

2. Transportation (car payments, gas, bus/train passes, Uber (if you have a car, do not include rideshare)

3. Food (groceries should be separated from takeout and restaurants).

4. Basic utilities (electricity, water, gas, basic internet).

5. Rainy day fund (savings are necessary to make sure that you don't need to call investments early).

The non-necessity category will have a lot more items. The first category should be debt. Debt should be broken into several categories:

1. Credit Cards
2. Personal loans or lines of credit
3. Student loans
4. Judgments or any other assessments, including taxes.

For many, this may be where most of your funds go. Other categories will include shopping, restaurant, and bar tabs.

Paying off high-interest debts and resolving any judgments, is necessary. While this may delay your initial investment plans, identifying areas where money is often wasted could help you redirect those funds into paying off your debts.

Once you have completed your financial audit, you can accurately assess where you are. The following scenarios will help you properly gauge where you are:

Scenario 1: If you have money left over each month or have been able to identify areas where you can streamline your extra spending, you can begin accumulating those funds in a separate account.

Depending on what that amount is per month, you may be ready to move to more active ways to build wealth in as little as 30-90 days.

Scenario 2: If you have high-interest debts and extra spending, you can pay down the highest interest debt with your other non-essential spending and start your investor fund in 60-180 days.

This is highly dependent upon how aggressive you are with managing and paying off your debt.

Scenario 3: If you have high-interest debt and no extra spending, you will need to continue on a debt reduction pathway before investing. If you are in this scenario, you may need to wait 12 months before fully embarking on the wealth journey.

Scenario 4: If you are spending more than you are bringing in, an effective spending reduction plan should be enacted before taking further wealth building steps.

After conducting your audit if you are still coming up short. Here are a few tips to help grow your savings.

Pay Yourself First

In the budget that you create aim to put something away each pay period. Most experts will tell you to aim to save 10 to 15 percent of your income, but make sure you start to reinforce the pattern. If you are receiving direct deposit, try having a set amount automatically placed in a savings account. Most people find it easier to save if they never see the money in their checking account.

Tip: Think about setting up a savings account that is not connected to your checking account and that does not have an atm card. The harder you have to work to get to the funds the less likely it is that you will spend them.

Make sure you are finding ways to cut spending. There are often non-essentials that can be reduced. This does not necessarily mean that you have to endure self-induced poverty, but you may be able to move your services to other providers. Use your power as a consumer to get better deals. Cell phone companies have also become more cost effective. Many consumers have dumped their cable companies but beware of piling on the app. On average, most cord-cutters now pay for 3-4 streaming services. While individually, 7-15 dollars per month may not seem like much, but in 1 year, a single $15 account per month comes to $180. If you have four accounts, that's an extra $720 per year.

Other ideas for cutting everyday expenses:

Look for community events that reduce your entertainment budget. You might be surprised about what your city has to offer.

No Accidental Consumption

Don’t fall for the “freemium” trap. One of the easiest ways for companies to make money is to get you in the door with a free trial and then convert to a paid monthly subscription. Take a look to see what you might be paying for that you forgot. Cancel the subscriptions and that you don't use. You might even consider taking them off automatic renewal to make sure that you have direct oversight into how much those subscriptions are costing you.

Pump your Brakes

Wait a few days before making a nonessential purchase. The wait might help you to realize that you don't need that item. You might even forget completely about it.

Setting savings goals can really help you make head way. This will require you to think about the short, mid, and long-term future goals. Short term goals like creating an emergency fund or a new business fund can take 1-2 years of savings time. Make sure that your goals are achievable. Creating extremely ambitious goals that make you miserable will mean you will ditch the plan quickly.

Retirement Accounts

Alongside a savings account you should absolutely be planning for retirement. Retirement means different things to different people. The one common thread for retirement is the need for money. The amount of money you need will highly depend on the life you want to live. Do you want to travel the world and play golf or sit on the front porch and sip lemonade? To get an idea take some time and evaluate your current lifestyle or any bucket list items you might have. Since you have already worked out how much you monthly/annual spend multiply that by the years you expect to live. Keep in mind that according to the United Nations global life expectancy 76.2 years. Of course, geography and sex affect this number but other factors including socioeconomic status are a contributing factor. In the United States race also can be a factor in life expectancy. According to data gathered by the Centers for Disease Control life expectancy by race:

- Native Americans: 75.06 years
- African Americans: 75.54 years
- White Americans: 79.12 years
- Hispanic Americans: 82.89 years
- Asian Americans: 86.67 years

Therefore, if you plan to retire at the traditional age of 65 you may have 10-20 years on average to provide for.

To keep it simple let's, do some basic math:

Retire at age 65

Expect to live for 20 years

Current costs of living annually $60,000

85 years- 65 years = 20

20 years x $60,000= $1.2M

That is before you include inflation or the rising cost of healthcare or housing. A financial planner can help you determine what your needs really are.

So, what is the path to saving $1M+? A retirement account or long term-investing plan is the path you likely must travel.

There are several common account types: Individual retirement accounts (IRAs), Roth IRAs, and employer-sponsored accounts. The employer sponsored accounts include two types: defined contribution plans, such as 401(k)s, and traditional pensions or defined benefits plans. Assets held in IRA and defined contribution plans may have some tax benefits. The defined benefits plan guarantees a stream of income in retirement.

Black and Hispanic families are far less likely to have retirement accounts. One reason for gaps in participation in retirement accounts is that not all families are eligible to participate in an employer-sponsored retirement plan. This may because the employer does not offer a plan, or they are not full-time. If you are eligible contributing even a small amount to the plan can make a significant difference over time. If your employer offers a company match remember to not leave funds on the table. Since the funds are taken out of your pay pre-tax you may not feel the impact in your net check. While it may be tempting to make a withdraw from your 401k remember there may be significant tax penalties and borrowing from your future may not be worth it long-term.

For those that are self-employed there are lots of retirement plan options including: one-participant 401(k), SEP IRA, SIMPLE IRA, Keogh plan, traditional and Roth IRA.

One-Participant 401(k)

A one-participant 401(k), also known as the solo-401k. It is for sole proprietors with no employees, other than a spouse working for the business. The solo-401k looks like a traditional employer sponsored 401k. The major difference is you contribute as the employer and the employee which manas you may have a higher contribution limit when compared to other tax-advantaged plans. Total contributions to the plan must not exceed $58,000, or $64,000 for people age 50 or older as of 2021. These limits change so always be sure to know the changes each tax year. If your spouse is also an employee, they can also match this contribution. To establish an individual 401(k), a business owner has to work with a financial institution.

SEP IRA

A simplified employee pension or SEP IRA is type of traditional IRA. This is commonly thought to be the easiest plan to establish and operate, making it a good option for entrepreneurs. It also allows for one or more employees.

In a SEP IRA, only the employer contributes to the fund, not the employees. You can contribute up to 25% of your net earnings (defined as your annual profit minus your self-employment taxes), up to a maximum of $58,000 in 2021. You can choose to make a lump sum contribution or skip it. There is no annual funding requirement. While you do not have to contribute to the plan each year, if you have employees then when you do contribute, you will need to contribute for all of your eligible employees—up to 25% of their compensation, limited to $290,000 annually. A SEP can be set-up at a brokerage, but it may not be the most effective way to save.

SIMPLE IRA

A SIMPLE IRA or savings incentive match plan for employees is a hybrid between an IRA and a 401(k) plan and works best for small businesses: companies with 100 or fewer employees that might find other plans too expensive. The SIMPLE IRA follows the same investment, rollover, and distribution rules as a traditional IRA, but it has lower contribution thresholds. You can contribute up to a maximum of $13,500 plus an additional $3,000 if you are 50 or older in 2021. Employees can contribute along with employers, in the same annual amounts. As the employer, however, you are required to match dollar for dollar up to 3% of each participating employee's income to the plan each year or a fixed 2% contribution to every eligible employee's income even if they do not contribute. The SIMPLE IRA is funded by tax-deductible employer contributions and pretax employee contributions, like 401k. Early withdrawal penalties are 25% within the first two years of the plan. A financial institution can help you setup this plan.

Keogh Plan

The Keogh plan or more commonly referred as a qualified or profit-sharing plan is a complex plan for entrepreneurs but allows for the largest potential savings amount. This plan looks like a defined contribution plan because a fixed sum or percentage is contributed every pay period. For 2021, these plans are capped to a total contribution of $58,000 for the year. Another option, though, allows Keogh plans to be structured as defined-benefit plans. For 2021, the maximum annual benefit was set at $230,000 or 100% of the employee's compensation, whichever is lower. A business must not be incorporated and set up as a sole proprietorship, limited liability company (LLC), or partnership to use a Keogh. Contributions can be made on a pre-tax basis and you can implement a vesting schedule. These plans are mainly beneficial to high earners, especially the defined-benefit version, which allows greater contributions than any other plan. Setting up a Keogh plan can have hefty filing requirements so you will need help from several professionals including an accountant, investment advisor, or a financial institution. Due to complexity only certain brokerages offer these plans so your vendor choices may be limited.

Traditional or Roth IRA

You can start your own individual IRA. Both Roth and traditional IRAs are available to anyone with employment income, and that includes freelancers. Roth IRAs let you contribute after-tax dollars, while traditional IRAs let you contribute dollars pretax. For 2021, the maximum annual contribution is $6,000, $7,000 if you are age 50 or older, or your total earned income, whichever is less. If you had a retirement plan at a former employer such as a 401(k), 403(b), or 457(b) with a former employer, rolling these accounts into an IRA can be an effective way to manage the savings. Consolidating these accounts may also give you greater control over how you invest your money.

Chapter Summary/Key Takeaways

If you went through the steps in this chapter, then you should now fully understand your financial picture. In addition to knowing your sources of income you now know exactly where your money goes and what you are retaining. This is critical in helping to determine what you have to become a Black Angel—But remember alternative investing is in addition to retirement planning not a full substitute.

Personal Budgeting Template

Simple Budget			
How much money do you make per month? ___________			
Item	**Amount**		
Salary/Pay			
Any additional Income			
Dividends			
Total			
How much do you spend per month? ___________			
Item	**Amount**		
Bills			
Groceries			
Mortgage			
Credit cards			
Gas			
Laundry			
Car loan/payment			
Utilities			
Clothing			
Daycare			
Medical/Dental Insurance			
Savings			
Property taxes			
Other			

Total			
Income vs. Expenses			
Item	**Amount**		
Monthly income			
Monthly expenses			
Subtract the expenses from the income			

CHAPTER THREE: OWN IT!

Ownership

I'm not saying owning a home makes life some kind of blissful paradise, simply that it makes the difference between freedom and enslavement.

-Tana French

Homeownership is an effective way to build wealth especially for low-income families. For many people a home will likely be the largest and most expensive purchase that they will ever make. According to the 2019 Survey of Consumer Finances, the median homeowner has more household wealth than a renter, nearly 40 times as much ($254,900 compared to $6,270). This is not a simple cause and effect relationship however regardless of the income lever a homeowner is wealthier than a renter. Most homeowner wealth comes from housing for every income category except for the very top earners. At the lowest income category, 92 percent of total homeowner net worth is tied to the value of residential property.

The path to homeownership has historically been rocky for many people of color. As recently, as the great recession of 2008 we saw discriminatory policies that funneled borrowers of color into subprime loans even when they qualified for better terms.

As we look at the vacuums left in many communities of color it is imperative that we own more of the housing in the community. According to several studies' Black homeownership under the age of 35 is less than 20%. This percentage increases to 50% for Blacks between ages of 35-54. To help to build wealth we should seek to purchase homes in lower income neighborhoods. This includes not selling familial homes in "less desirable" areas of the city once a family member passes away. As the cost of housing continues to rise homeownership offers a way to create stability in your expenses because your mortgage costs are set for the life of the loan.

When considering homeownership many experts will suggest not immediately looking to purchase your dream home but rather choosing function over style. This might mean choosing a home that fits your basic needs and foregoing luxuries that drive up the prices. I would suggest looking at the long-term development plans for your city or municipality. This will help you to see where future infrastructural investments are coming. This can help you identify areas that will appreciate in value. Don't chase cranes. Often times if you see lots of cranes in an area then the prices are already becoming inflated. If you have already taken the ownership plunge and like the real estate market as your primary investment vehicle to provide additional income sure to not become over-extended (over-leveraged) in the housing market. Many real estate investors suffered losses that were hard to recover from because their real estate portfolio was not well balanced. If you have not taken the ownership plunge think about adding a home purchase to your purchase goals. Not sure if you are ready to buy consider these steps.

Debt is manageable

This may not mean that you are debt free. You may have some sort of debt including student loans, or a small amount of credit card debt. This could mean that you have funds to go towards a down payment.

Your Credit Score Is Improving

You will need solid credit to qualify for a home loan. You can qualify for most mortgages with a credit score of at least 620. If you do not know your credit score, make sure to pull your credit report and know your numbers. There are usually many programs that can help improve your credit so make sure to not count yourself out.

Steady Income

If you have consistent income this may be incredibly attractive to lenders. Generally, there is not a specific minimum income needed to buy a house. You will need to have a lender let you know how much house you can afford. There are several online calculators however to get a proper answer you should work with a professional. A number called your DTI or Debt-to-Income ratio. This is a calculation of how much you owe versus how much you make. Most lenders prefer borrowers with a DTI under 50%.

One final note on ownership. Remember when preparing to take this step you will need to consider all of the costs associated with ownership, including property taxes. A few costs to keep in mind include:

Insurance

This is a must even if your mortgage lender does not require it. An act of God or other accident can spell financial ruin if there is no insurance.

Property taxes

No matter where you live you must pay property taxes. Property taxes are calculated as a percentage of your home's value. The more your home is worth, the more you'll pay.

Closing costs

Closing costs are due one-time when you close your loan. They cover things like the title insurance, attorney fees, lender fees and more. You can expect to pay 3% – 6% of your total loan value in closing costs. There may be homebuyer programs that can help alleviate some of these costs.

Maintenance

If you are the owner, then there is no maintenance number to call. Those costs are now your responsibility. Having a savings account that can absorb these costs is important. The repair costs on an older home can be higher so make sure you ask questions when you are having the home inspected. If large costs like a roof or HVAC system are near the end of their life span, you may be able to have the purchase price reduced or the owner may be willing to have it repaired. You never know if you don't ask.

Chapter Summary/Key Takeaways

Ownership especially land and home ownership aid in wealth building in a way that few other items can. Having real property builds equity. It is tangible asset that can be borrowed against if needed and it can be passed to your children. Remember the goal of ownership is to have an asset that increases in value, not just having something that is impressive to others. Start small (if necessary) and grow from there.

CHAPTER FOUR: WHAT THE FUTURE HOLDS

Planning

"A goal without a plan is just a wish."

Antoine de Saint-Exupéry

The final piece to the wealth building puzzle is planning. Planning is what enables the building of generational wealth. It is what sets the entire community up for success. Planning comes in several different forms: Insurance, Retirement, Educational, and Estate. Each of these financial tools are important for a well-rounded portfolio.

Insurance

Remember the play by Lorraine Hanesberry, *A Raisin in the Sun?* The play showcases the importance of leaving the legacy via insurance. Each member of the family sees the potential differently. The mother wanted to buy a home, the son wanted to invest in a business, and the daughter saw medical school come into reach. They were all correct. The unexpected capital into the family could help transform the future. Insurance comes in several forms. In this section we will primarily be speaking about life insurance but remember that car, home, and health insurance are all important to have to make sure that when the unexpected happens it does leave you drowning in bills. There are a lot of life insurance products and it can be difficult to understand how much coverage you need, the difference between whole and term life. Let's start at the beginning. Life insurance falls into 3 categories: term insurance, permanent insurance, or a hybrid insurance.

Term Life Insurance

Term life insurance provides coverage at with consistent payment for a limited period of time or the relevant term. After the term expires, coverage at the previous rate of premiums is no longer guaranteed. The client may have to repurchase coverage with a separate set of conditions. If the life insured dies during the term, a death benefit may be paid to the named beneficiary. Term insurance can be one of the least expensive ways to purchase a substantial death benefit when the premium amount and coverage amount is taken into consideration. It is important to note that data suggest that less than 1% of term life insurance policies pay out, possibly because the insured may outlive the policy term, so buyer beware.

Permanent Life Insurance

Permanent life insurance is general term for life insurance policies that do not have an expiration date. Usually, permanent life insurance combines a death benefit with some form of savings.

There are two types of permanent life insurance: whole life and universal life. Whole life insurance provides coverage for the full lifetime of the insured, and a savings that can grow at a guaranteed rate. Universal life insurance also offers a savings element in addition to a death benefit, but it may have different types of premium structures and increases in value based on how the stock market performs. While it may be obvious this form of life insurance is not permanent if you stop paying the premiums.

Understanding Permanent Life Insurance Cash Value

When you pay your monthly premium, a portion goes to maintaining the policy's death benefit and a portion goes to building cash value. As this value builds the policy owner may be able to borrow against that cash value and some policies may allow you to withdraw cash for certain purposes like covering medical expenses or paying for a child's college education. In most cases there is a waiting period to access the cash value (this allows the value to build over time) so do not think of this policy as a checking account. One final note if you borrow against the cash value and you pass away then the loan will be paid FIRST and any remaining value will be paid to the beneficiaries. If the debt is more than the policy's value, then there may be no payout or coverage. There may also be tax benefits, as the growth of the cash value it may be tax-deferred. This means that the policyholder pays no taxes on any earnings as long as the policy is active.

Universal Life Insurance

Universal life is blend term and permanent life insurance plans. These policies can be a bit confusing if not well written. Be sure to work with a reputable licensed insurance professional and understand the design of your policy and what your benefits are.

Life insurance is a key component of wealth building. Leaving a death benefit can mean that your children (or the next generation) do not incur debt for your final expenses, and they end up with additional capital for their savings or investments. Think of it as an effortless way to create trust fund babies.

Estate Planning

Do I need a Will?

It may be very easy to think that you don't have enough to pay much attention to writing a will. Many don't recognize that if you pass away without a will then state will decide what happens to your assets, according to the laws of your state. As a practical matter, you should be sure to write down your final wishes. Grief can alter decision making, so make things easier on your loved ones. A death letter can be instrumental in organizing your thoughts. For example, do you have a particular type of service in mind? Burial costs have accelerated and can be upwards of $8,500 in the most modest of circumstances. In the letter, in addition to being able to leave loving thoughts, you can leave your bank account information including atm pin numbers, you can let your family know what insurance policies you may have and where to find them. You can even make it known who should receive particular items. This letter can be placed on record with the estate division of the court. You must be of sound mind and the letter must be signed and dated. This guidance is a good start towards making your wishes known. A will creates more formality and can reduce the likelihood that a family member may challenge your wishes. However, to the law your last will and testament does not have to be drafted by an attorney to be honored.

Money Saving Tip: If possible, purchase your burial plot early or buy in bulk (*not a joke*). Burial plot costs are not immune to inflation or demand pricing. A plot will cost you more if you need it immediately versus if you are pre-planning. There is also a pre-owned market. No, they are not occupied, the original purchaser may have had a change in plans, like a divorce and no longer need the plot.

Advance Directives

Many people may not recognize this terminology but have

likely been asked about these if you have ever needed serious medical care. An advanced directive gives insights into what medical decisions you want made in the event you can not communicate them. A living will instruct health care professionals what to do in specific situations. For example, do you want to be resuscitated should your heart stop? A Do Not Resuscitate (DNR) instructs health professionals to not use CPR or other means to restart your heart. You may also decide that you do not wish to be kept alive if you enter a vegetative state. Be sure to designate a health care proxy, or another person you trust, to make decisions for you. When made in advance, these decisions made can have direct implications on your wealth. Healthcare costs, especially at the end of life, can costs millions and leave a substantial amount of debt. Every person is different, and your position may change over your lifetime.

Trust

Often, we associate trust with trust fund, and we image a very wealthy family. A trust is simple a legal tool that allows a third party to hold your assets and a trustee to direct those assets. Trusts, along with a will, can help protect your assets from creditors and lawsuits. There may also be reductions in estate and gift taxes when a trust is used. Trusts can be instrumental for someone looking to create generational wealth. A trust can guide how assets are disbursed to children or a family member who may be too young or immature to handle the money. This can mean there are age milestones before funds are transferred or monthly disbursements to control spending. This can also be stipulations like graduated from college, getting married, or having children. There are several types of trusts be two types that get discussed often are: revocable and irrevocable trusts. A revocable trust is a living document it can be changed, amended, or even dissolved as long as the person who created it is alive. This type of trust becomes irrevocable at death. An irrevocable trust cannot be changed. Once the conditions are set that it—so no take backs. As with any legal or financial tool a qualified estate attorney and financial planner should be consulted to help you determine the type of trust that is right for you.

Estate Planning is a complex field. There are a considerable number of techniques that can be deployed to reduce tax penalties, administrative costs, and enable the transfer of assets before death.

Educational Planning

If you have children in your life whether biological or otherwise one of the best things you can do for them is starting an educational savings account. Note that I did not call it a college savings plan because there are multiple paths including trade schools that may be in that child's future. Starting the account sooner rather than later is always the best advice. According to data reported to U.S. News in an annual survey, the average tuition for the 2019-2020 school year ranged from $41,426 (for private colleges) to $11,260 (for state colleges). That is per year so putting a dent in the amount that the student must borrow can really set the child up for success as they will not start adulthood drowning in debt.

529 Plan

This is the most common savings plan discussed with parents. A 529 is savings plans, usually sponsored by state governments, that encourages saving for future education costs. They offer tax-friendly benefits as you may be able to deduct your contributions from your state income taxes and when you withdraw the money for the child's education, the money will not be taxed. Opening an account generally does not require much money for example in North Carolina you can open a 529 for as little as $25.

Savings Bonds

Savings bonds can offer incredibly low risk as they are backed by the government. They also will also offer low returns, as an annual fixed rate can be in the range of 0.010%. If you redeem a savings bond and use it for some educational costs, there may be additional tax benefits.

Coverdell Education Savings Account

The Coverdell Education Account is a tax-deferred trust account that can be used for education from elementary through higher education, including room and board. The earnings grow tax-free, and distributions are not charged income taxes if the funds are used for educational purposes. These funds must be used before the age of 30 or there may be tax penalties- so no career students.

Chapter Summary/Key Takeaways

In this chapter we covered planning from sunrise to sunset. It can be uncomfortable discussing these topics, but we must begin having these discussions before the unexpected happens. It is never too late to start the planning process. Now that we have a solid financial foundation, we can begin covering the basics of becoming an angel investor.

PART II: TRYING ON YOUR WINGS

"Angels come in all shapes and size—find a pair of wings that fit you and fly."

- Dr. Shante

Every investor started somewhere. To become an investor, you have to make your first investment but before you can begin the journey, you must first know where you are.

In this second part, we will discuss:

- Basic terminology
- How to assess where you are
- Preparing your finances for investing
- How to identify what to invest in
- How to seek out the right investments

CHAPTER FIVE: THE BASICS

Capital is the lifeblood of a business. Even the most prosperous businesses need capital injections every now and then to drive growth. One of the easiest ways for businesses, especially startups, to raise capital is to turn to venture capital firms or Angel investors. But for Black entrepreneurs, raising capital via these sources is almost impossible. Statistically speaking, the odds are stacked against African American entrepreneurs. For instance, reports by CB Insights revealed that only about 1% of Black founders of tech companies receive venture capital funding. African American business owners also have a harder time securing loans from banks and traditional financial institutions because many of them are not keen on lending money to minorities. As a result, African Americans lose out on opportunities to thrive economically, create more employment opportunities for the Black community, and bridge the wealth gap for people of color.

A report released by The Center for Global Policy Solutions revealed that "*there are over 1 million businesses that could be pro-*

duced by people of color, but are stunted due to socially discriminating financing practices, and a bias towards companies run largely by White men."

Jessica Norwood, the Founder of The Runway Project Initiative, an organization working to create solutions for addressing the wealth gap impeding minority business growth revealed that "*Many Black entrepreneurs turn to credit cards or moonlighting under part-time or full-time jobs to pad the growth of their business. This bootstrapping method offers drips of money but makes it much more difficult and time-consuming to access much larger capital.*"

A lot of Black business owners, because they cannot access traditional funding like their White counterparts, are left with no choice but to turn to more accessible funding like credit cards, which often comes with exorbitant interest rates that sometimes can be difficult to manage. They often end up with huge debt burden and get pushed further down the rabbit hole of poor credit scores, business collapse, liquidation, and generational poverty. Some potential founders, not willing to take the risk, simply dump their business ideas and take up paid employment instead.

We owe it to our communities and the future generations to put an end to these socially discriminating financing practices that is making it difficult for the African American business community to grow, thrive, and create any sustainable generational wealth. We have to step in to save our African American business community and give Black founders and business owners the opportunity that they are consistently being denied. The only way we can do this is by becoming investors ourselves.

Only about 1.3% of Angel investors in the United States are African Americans, and this might explain why many Black business owners and founders continue to be marginalized and discriminated against. If we as African Americans participate more in investing- become Angel Investors ourselves, then we will be able to give more African Americans the platform to raise capital for their businesses, generate wealth, and create sustainable wealth for the future generations.

One reason why there are so few Black Angel investors is because of the common misconception that you have to be a millionaire or be very wealthy to become an investor- No, you don't have to. In fact, with as little as $2,000, you can get started as an individual Angel investor, and with as little as $500, you can join an angel investment group, and invest collectively with other Black Angels. Imagine thousands of African Americans coming together and pooling small amounts of money together for investments- it quickly adds up and can make a significant difference in our community.

For most beginner investors, the terms and terminology can be daunting. Every investment category has its lingo, but there are some underlying basics that you should know.

Who Is An Angel Investor?

An Angel investor, also known as a private investor, seed investor, or angel funder, is generally a high net worth individual who provides financial backing for small startups or entrepreneurs. This type of Investor is looking for ownership in the startup in exchange for the cash.

The symbolism of an angel is very appropriate. Usually, an angel is investing money when the company is not generating revenue and needs a miracle because they are in a slow or difficult phase in the company's life.

Angel investors are typically not looking to be involved in the day-to-day operations of the company, and an angel investor does not have to be an accredited investor; however, many are. This is where the opportunity for everyone to participate in investing lies as there is no minimum investment for an angel investor. Even though the average investment for an angel investment is approximately $75,000, DO NOT let this discourage you as this number varies widely depending on what region of the country you occupy.

Types Of Angel Investors: What Type Of Investor Am I?

There are many names for investors. Luckily, many of them mean the same things:

- **Seed investor**- this is a reference to where the company is in its lifecycle. A seed investor typically invests in business at the startup or beginning phase of the business.
- **Venture capitalist**- is an investor who provides capital to firms that exhibit high growth potential in exchange for an equity stake. This Investor is generally associated with a particular firm or fund.
- **Passive Investor**- an investor who does not par-

ticipate in the day-to-day operations of the company (*there are other definitions as it relates to stocks or mutual funds*)

- **Active Investor**- an investor who takes a hands-on approach to investment. These types of investors are often involved in decision making, or in the day to day running of the business.

Accredited Versus Non-Accredited

Federal law defines those who can participate in certain types of investments. These rules are intended to ensure that the persons investing in an opportunity can accept the risks of loss and are also able to remain financially stable afterwards.

The definition of an accredited investor is very specific. You are an accredited investor if:

- Your earned income exceeds $200,000 (or $300,000 together with a spouse) in each of the two years prior, and is reasonably expected to remain the same for the current year,

OR

- You have a net worth of over $1 million, either alone or together with a spouse (excluding the value of your primary residence).

An accredited investor could also be:

- Any trust, with total assets above $5 million, not formed specifically to purchase the subject securities, whose purchase is directed by a sophisticated person,

OR

• Any entity in which all of the equity owners are accredited investors. If you fit into any of the above criteria, then you qualify as an accredited investor.

While there is no official place to register as an accredited investor, many companies or entities will have you self-declare that you meet the criteria. They may also request proof of your financial status.

A non-accredited investor is anyone who does not meet the criteria above. Most Americans fall into the non-accredited investor bucket.

Most accredited investors have many investment advice options, so I will be focusing on the non-accredited investor majority.

Venture Investment Or Main Street Investment

Venture investments include the flashy new technologies and gadgets that people associate with Silicon Valley. Think about the next Facebook or I-phone. These businesses are called high growth companies and are often associated with new and cutting-edge technology and/or business models. These businesses can create multi-millionaires overnight, but they are also very risky. Predicting the wave of the future is more complicated than many think. It often takes more than 5 years to see these startups start to generate returns for their early investors.

Main street businesses, on the other hand, are the businesses that we utilize every day: restaurants, meat markets, fish markets, daycares, beauty supply stores, food trucks, hotels/ motels, and the list goes on. All of these businesses can generate outsized revenue, grow, and scale with the right amount of capital.

Angel investors can make a significant difference in these businesses as well. These businesses are revenue-generating and may be able to provide returns to their investors in as little as one month.

It is essential to know how you wish to make a difference as an investor.

Contrary to popular belief, venture investment and main street investment are of equal importance, and both can create economic power for its owners.

Understanding Your Role as an Angel Investor

Now that you understand some of the investment lingo as it relates to angel investing, let's talk about what your role as an angel investor will be.

The term 'Angel' came from the Broadway Theater when wealthy people were known to give money to theater companies to fund productions.

This might explain why most people believe that an angel investor's role begins and ends with signing and handing out large checks, but it goes beyond that.

An Angel investor's role in a company goes beyond capital participation- Angel investors also add value to the business in diverse ways including but not limited to performance monitoring, coaching, providing sales leads, and overseeing the operations of the business.

As an Angel investor, you are probably a successful entrepreneur or a successful career man or woman yourself, and the knowledge and wealth of experience that you can bring to the business may even be more important than the cash. A business with a lot of money to spend, but without a clear-cut strategy to utilize the funds optimally may still fail.

It's okay if you would prefer to play the role of a passive investor (because frankly, most angel investors rarely participate), but it is important to keep in mind that your returns are completely hinged on the success of the business – the more successful the business, the more profits you earn on your investment.

Studies have shown that businesses whose angel investors played active roles in the business are more likely to succeed than businesses whose investors simply signed the checks and took the back burner.

One study even showed that angel investors who interacted with their invested companies received at least three times more return than angel investors who did not.

As an Angel investor, you can play various roles in helping your invested business succeed. Let's take a look at five typical ways that you can participate in a business as an angel investor:

Coach/Mentor: Angel investors may also play the role of mentor or coach.

They may give regular advice or inputs that can help to move the business forward.

If you've spent years working in the Pharmaceutical industry for instance, and you're investing in a business that is also operating within the same industry, you would likely know more about how to navigate the waters compared to a set of newcomers.

The business can always take advantage of your connections, your experience, and your knowledge to move forward.

Sometimes, businesses have to hire the services of a consultant when charting unfamiliar territories and that would cost them a lot of money- what if you can step in and offer your services as a consultant and help the business save costs? This will go a long way in increasing the business's profit and invariably, your own returns.

Team Member: In addition to providing financial investment, you can also play a part-time role in the business such as serving on the board of directors or serving in other capacities.

Reserve Force: You can be a passive investor who is also willing to help the entrepreneur on an as-needed basis. If the entrepreneur encounters some challenges, you can step in and help them solve the problem or provide valuable insights that can help them navigate the waters.

Unofficial Marketer: This is one of the easiest extra roles that you can play as an Angel investor.

Every business craves more sales and revenue, and you can help your invested companies in this aspect by helping to spread the word about the business to your friends, family, to your network and groups you belong, or to your social media connections.

Financial Consultant: This is one aspect where a lot of entrepreneurs, especially startups, run into challenges.

I have seen startup founders with smart business ideas but zero idea on how to manage the financial aspects of their businesses, especially the working capital management and taxation aspects of their businesses.

While some larger or established businesses may be able to hire the services of professional Accountants or Tax Consultants to help them with the books, the mom-and-pop businesses and startups can do with some professional help and experience that comes free of charge.

These are only some of the typical ways that you can add value to your invested company as an Angel investor. In fact, this is one of the things that make the difference between an Angel and a Traditional Investor.

A Traditional Investor is only about his money- all he cares about is to see his investment portfolio double in size. He doesn't really care how the company does it, or how the business impacts the community.

But an angel is more of a humanitarian- you know that if this little business is able to thrive, a lot of people can benefit. The business can create employment for the unemployed, bring improvement to the community, and create generational wealth, so you don't just put in money; you contribute in whatever ways you can to drive the growth and success of the business.

Of course, you are not Santa Claus- your major goal is to make some profits, but you do it bearing in mind that this business is more than just a money spinner.

Your participation will of course be subject to the disposition of the business owner. Some entrepreneurs may not be open to the idea of an investor participating in their businesses beyond capital provision. In that case, it's okay to take a backseat but you can just let them know how you can be of help, and that they shouldn't hesitate to reach out if they ever need help in those aspects of their business.

Investment Terms

While some terms are unique to venture investments, there are some common terms for both types of investments.

To help navigate which terms belong to which category, here is a quick color code:

Violet=Venture Investments

Blue=Main street Investments

Black= Both Types

Startup Financing Cycle

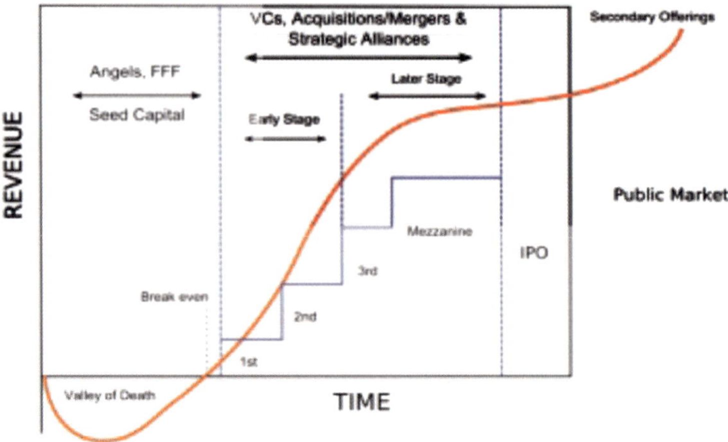

Company Stages

There are several stages of a startup:

Concept stage- This is also known as the idea stage.

At this stage, the startup has not solidified many key elements of the business, such as how the business will make money, who the target customers are, the product, and so on.

At this stage, a company is generally not ready for investors and should be self-funding or bootstrapping the concept.

This is not the stage for angel investors because this stage does not have enough "meat on the bones" to make an investment-wise.

Note: many new investors fall victim to the back of the napkin success story. While this has happened in history, it is not a common story. Do not fall for quickly drawn ideas—save those investments for your billionaire years.

Pre-Seed- This stage is when a startup begins to test and validate the ideas that they decided on in the concept stage.

This could mean building a "proof of concept" to demonstrate the product or conducting potential customer surveys to determine if they would be interested in the product or service.

I don't generally advise angels to invest at this stage unless the startup has a "prototype" built, and they have at least some indication of interest from potential consumers.

Seed- This stage is where the startup has a viable concept and is looking to gain traction.

This is where angel investors begin to appear. Angel capital may be used to complete the prototype or to aid in gaining early traction.

Early Stage- This stage is really where a company starts its journey.

At his stage the company has had its concept tested and vetted and has refined the product based on the results. The product is ready to be introduced to the broader target market, and revenue *should* begin to be generated.

Angel investments are particularly critical at this stage because to generate revenue, several things need to be invested in, including marketing, inventory, and sales.

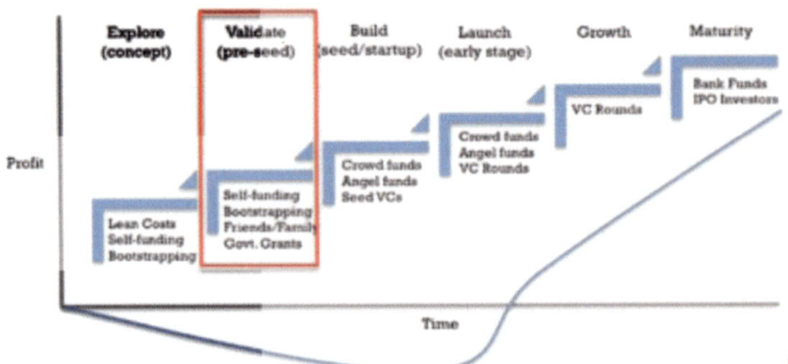

Growth and Mature Stage- These stages generally require more capital, and most angel investors don't have the money to contribute at this stage.

Note: If you decide to invest in established businesses within your community, they will likely be in the mature stage. These anchor businesses are the lifeblood of communities, and many would benefit from angels coming to their rescue.

The angel sweet spot for venture investment is in the pre-seed, seed, and early-stage phases of a business.

For main street investments, it is mostly the growth and mature stage; however, there may be opportunities to invest in a known market with a new location or concept moving into a new market.

The entrepreneurs may be new to business ownership and should be treated more like an unproven venture investment.

Marketing/Money Terms

Revenue- This is money generated from product sales.

This is different from profit. Profit is money left after all overhead and product or company costs are deducted. Most of the investments that angel investors make are not in companies that are generating profit.

Return on Investment (ROI) - Simply put, this is what you get back for your money.

If you are an investor, you are looking to make more than what you put in, and what you get as reward for your investments is called your Return on Investment (ROI).

Return is calculated in multiples. A 1x return means you got your money back, while 2x means you got double, 3X means you got three times what you invested, etc.

It's also possible to make negative returns known as a loss. This is often expressed in percentages, but the same math applies.

Convertible Notes- A convertible note is often used in the investment industry.

The funds from the Investor are treated as a loan, meaning the funds collect interest at a specified rate, and this interest is paid after an agreed period.

If the company cannot return the investment and the interest within the term of the note, then that note converts to ownership in the company, generally at a pre-determined conversion price.

Convertible notes allow the startup to get investments in without giving too much ownership early in the startup's life.

Convertible notes are a good option for investors as they allow funds to collect interest. They may also pay out at regular intervals and offer the ability to gain ownership at a lower price.

Not all convertible notes have a voluntary conversion. This means that after a specified period, the Investor may gain ownership stake regardless of the payment.

Due Diligence- This involves investigating all the assumptions and validating any statements that the company or business owner has made.

You should question everything that's presented. The more information you have, the more informed you can be about how your money would be used.

Valuation- This is what the company is worth.

Valuations at the early stages are often not very reliable especially if there is no revenue being generated, and the business has not received any other investments.

It is crucial to understand how the company reached its numbers and a valuation will give you an insight into what the company is truly worth.

Equity- This is the amount of ownership you receive in exchange for the investment, and this number may be a very small percentage.

It is unrealistic for an angel investor to expect equal (50%) or controlling (>50%) ownership. It is important to understand that requiring large stakes to be given at an early stage could inhibit the company from fundraising in the future, and that will inhibit the value of your stake.

Traction- This could come in two forms: money being generated from sales, or early customer acquisition.

I generally don't put much stock in traction that is free use or sign-up interest. This is because converting free customers to paid customers is not as easy a feat as most startups believe.

Exit- This is the time when the investor "cashes out" of an investment.

Exit events come in many different forms: cash outs, merger, bankruptcy, Initial Public Offering, Acquisition.

Scaling- simply stated, this means that a business is prepared to grow to a new level.

Growth has to be enabled. If a business generates more sales but is unable to fill those orders or service all the new clients, the business could fail.

Growth requires planning, funding, systems and processes, proper staff levels, adequate technology, and sometimes, more partners.

Chapter Summary/Key Takeaways

In this chapter, we reviewed the basic terminology. While investment may require its own dictionary, the basics to know are: what kind of Investor am I, and how will I make my money back.

In the next chapter, you will be able to articulate this and pinpoint your angel characteristics.

CHAPTER SIX: FINDING GOLD

Before you decide where to invest, you have to decide on what type of business interests you.

If you are working with a smaller investment budget, or simply looking to impact your community, then main street businesses may be the type of business you want to invest in.

These businesses are likely in staple industries like food/markets/restaurants, funeral homes, exterminators, car washes, flower shops, barbershops, or beauty salons.

Main street businesses may pose less risk to investors as they are already revenue-generating and have a consumer base. These types may be seeking capital to expand inventory, add a new product line, or renovate their properties.

If you are more interested in investing in new products or new ideas, then you should be looking at startups.

Startups are riskier investments, but they often offer higher return potential compared to main street investments. While many people worry about not having anything to invest in, in my experience, once the word gets out that you have money to invest (even if it's a small amount), you will be inundated with "opportunities".

There are lots of ways to identify potential investments but before you begin accepting and evaluating opportunities, it is essential to decide what you want to invest in.

How To Decide What To Invest In

I suggest making a list of the areas that you have expertise in, and your areas of interest. Never invest in things or industries that you don't know or understand no matter how hot the topic is, or what social media pundits are touting as the next big thing.

Expertise has very little to do with having learned something in school, or it being your job or career, your expertise may also come from personal experience.

For example, if you know hair salons based on your spending habits, or if you are a pet lover and have insights about pet products - that could be an excellent place to start.

While this may not strike you as expertise, you likely know more than you think about operations.

This is not to say that you should exclude topics that you studied in school or ignore your career. I have found that investing is as much a science as it is an art. If you have both passion and experience, you may be able to develop what I call an 'investment gut.' Your investment gut will allow you to quickly decipher when something does not ring true, or when an opportunity just doesn't sound right.

Once you have narrowed your topics, then you can begin to look into external sources. These may include articles, news reports, or blogs that speak to trends within an industry. If you decide to invest in something you don't know much about, you must educate yourself properly.

For example, many people find themselves interested in investing in real estate, cryptocurrency, or cannabis because of online chatter. Many reality shows and influencers may give a false impression of how easy it is to earn a return. I have seen many people think that they can "flip" a house or buy bitcoin and be millionaires in no time.

It is important to keep in mind that Investing is not a get rich quick scheme. If you are looking to invest in a trendy topic, you will need to spend considerable time in the preparation stage to make sure that you have a strong foundation about the market - where it has been and where it is going.

I suggest narrowing your initial investment interest to no more than two. Preferably, the interests should occupy the same industry category. Once you've gotten your bearings, you can now begin to diversify.

How To Seek Out The Right Investors

Seek, and You Shall Find

Now that we are all so interconnected- thanks to the internet- turning on your investor sign is easier than ever. However, a social media announcement may not be the best method for sourcing opportunities.

There are a number of smart ways to seek out investment opportunities with good potential.

Let's split investments into two buckets: main street businesses and startups.

Main Street Businesses

If you are seeking to make a more immediate impact in your community, invest in established businesses.

Here are a few ways to find good main street investment opportunities:

"A Place Where Everybody Knows Your Name."

Start with places you already patronize that align with your area of interest. You can start some with basic surveillance- as a customer/ patron, look for ways in which your experience could be more enjoyable.

Do you love the product but dislike the service?

Are they always out of stock on your favorite item?

Would you love to stay inside the facility, but it's not very inviting?

Are there products that you consume that you wish you could buy and take home?

These are all areas of opportunities; opportunities that all require some capital investment.

Most mom-and-pop small businesses stay afloat but may not have the margins to cover payroll, overhead, and money to reinvest. Start by striking up a conversation with the owner, let them know about your observations.

Many owners have thought about the same improvements but lack the access to capital to make it happen whether through profit or loan from financial institutions.

If the owner is open to the discussion, let them know that you may be potentially interested in investing in the business. The owner's reply will be indicative of whether they are open to discussion or not. Keep in mind that not all businesses want an investor or a partner, and it is not your job to convince them that it's a good idea. A partner that is easy to work with will make your life easier and give your investment the best opportunity to thrive. If the answer is no, continue to patronize the business and keep building a relationship with the employees and the owners. Once a relationship has been established, then they may be more open to working with you.

Remember, build a relationship—once you have planted the idea of an investment, you don't have to bring it up again. A genuine relationship will get you farther.

"The Smoky Backrooms."

Business associations are a great way to learn about opportunities. These associations may be trade groups, neighborhood coalitions, neighborhood business owner groups, or local chambers of commerce (especially the smaller affiliate chambers).

These groups host meetings and educational sessions that can bring many issues to the forefront. However, access to capital is a mainstay for many of these groups.

If you are unsure where to begin, then start with a specific program or activity. I suggest a program that is focused on access to capital. That way, you know that you are in the room with lots of people who are seeking investment. Another way to get a full lay of the land is to volunteer. By volunteering, you are building a relationship with the group, and this will give you first-hand knowledge of the neighborhood- *and the neighbors are always chatting.*

When in these rooms, don't be shy about introducing yourself as someone interested in investing in the community. Those that are interested will follow-up.

There is no need to rush to sign-up for full membership of any of these groups; try out the group well before you make a membership investment.

"Your Friendly Neighborhood Banker."

If you have not already done so as a part of your financial audit when opening your investment account, then meet with your banker.

Small business bankers are well-tuned into the community. I always recommend having an account with a community bank or a credit union. These banks are generally more intimately ingrained into the community as opposed to their big-box counterparts.

They see businesses of all stripes and levels seeking capital via loans or lines of credit, often having to deny them, or turn them away because they don't meet the lending criteria.

While they will not be able to give you customer details, you can provide them with the leeway to share your information or introduce such customers.

Higher Education

In recent years, the Small Business Administration (SBA) has partnered with local colleges or Universities to create Small Business Development Centers (SBDC's).

These centers were established to provide business-related assistance and knowledge to help entrepreneurs start, run, and grow their businesses. These services are often offered at a low cost or free of charge.

While they act as a tremendous resource, they often lack the capital to help many businesses with needs that extend beyond education or programming.

Across the United States and Puerto Rico, there are nearly 1,000 SBDC's.

Find one close to you and make an appointment with one of the center's representatives. Tell them what you are looking to invest in. They will likely know of many businesses that need capital.

Startups

A startup is a new business that is less than five years old by most definitions.

According to the SBA, over 627,000 businesses are started each year so you will have no problems finding investment opportunities. Research shows that startups in accounting, online retail, construction, and landscaping were most likely to get started with under $5,000 in startup costs (Trends, n.d.). However, if you are going to invest in startups, I suggest having at least $10,000 in capital.

This may seem like a lot of savings; however, if after your financial audit you were able to save $27.40 every day for one year, you will have $10,000 individually to invest.

This number is reduced if you are a part of a collective group; an investment group of 30 with each member investing $822 will get the group to $10,000 quickly.

In addition to the suggestions above, there are several avenues for identifying startup investment opportunities.

Crowdfunding

Crowdfund raisers help startups reach their capital goals by collecting small amounts from large groups. There are two types of crowdfunding campaigns- those that raise equity, and those that give in-kind products or promotional items in exchange for investments. You should only consider those campaigns raising equity if you want a financial return.

Crowdfunding campaigns are usually hosted on platforms that are regulated, and the terms of the deal are pre-determined. Often, these campaigns are for startups with technology components, but they represent many industries.

Depending on the campaign, minimum contributions can be as low as $100.

Pitch Competitions

A lot of startups turn to pitch competitions to raise capital and hone their pitching skills. Many of these competitions are open to the public and allow you to hear about the companies and hear the expert judges.

While there will be a winner announced, that doesn't necessarily mean that it is the best company, so feel free to reach out to whichever concept or founders most resonate with you. To right-size the best potential investment, choose competitions with prizes that are similar to your investment size.

Business Or Technology Conferences

These are conferences are typically aimed at new startups.

While the program itself may not particularly be of interest to you, the demonstration day or the exhibitor space should be. Attending or participating in these components of the conference is usually free and allows the startup to set up a booth and interact with the public. This is your opportunity to meet founders and discuss potential investment opportunities.

Social Media

Social media is by far, my least favorite way of discovering an investment opportunity. However, many people are more comfortable in cyberspace.

I do not recommend that you create a post saying you have money that you want to invest for many reasons.

Here are my suggested tips for finding opportunities via social media: In the headline portion of your social media page, describe yourself as an investor, and define the industry you are interested in.

Those looking for investors will find you as they search for specific profile descriptors. This method works best on LinkedIn, Instagram, and Twitter.

Be careful with opening random links and attachments on social media and avoid giving out any personal information.

Chapter Summary/Key Takeaways

There are many opportunities to get involved as an investor. In this chapter, we discuss many novel ways to find investment opportunities.

Some other considerations before you start your search:

- Create a separate email account that is dedicated to sending and receiving investment information.
- Pull in several opportunities; don't let your investment money burn a hole in your pocket.

Many venture capital firms see more than 1000 opportunities in a year. Cast your net wide.

- Stick to the area that you decided to invest in. Don't get distracted by other opportunities that are off base.
- While you are looking for opportunities, keep your funds separate and continue to build the account as you are gathering information.

If you have created a strong relationship with your banker, they will have likely set you up with an account that collects some interest. Even if a small amount- it is usually worth it.

Do not have an ATM card issued on the account and do not connect it to your other accounts.

Remember, learning about the opportunities is not a second job but an enjoyable experience. If you have chosen an area that you enjoy, you will be able to learn more about the industry. Focus on building a relationship, and the opportunities will be endless.

PART III: THE MORE YOU KNOW

"Risk comes from not knowing what you are doing."

-WARREN BUFFET

In this section we will discuss how to evaluate potential opportunities. We will discuss:

- How to Vet a Business or Idea Before You Invest
- Preparing for due diligence
- Which documents to request
- Holistic evaluation
- Setting expectations
- A making a selection
- Deciding how much return is acceptable

CHAPTER SEVEN: DEEP DIVE PREP

In my experience, the diving line between a lousy investment and a smart one is the amount of due diligence that is conducted before investing. While diligence does not guarantee you a return, it does equip you with information that will help you make a wise decision. Remember, due diligence is merely an investigation process. At this stage, you have to think of yourself as an investment detective. When seeking investors, every business will show you its best qualities. You will likely only hear about the upside and how great things are going. It becomes up to you to find the warts, expose the weaknesses, and identify the risks and other points of failure.

I have seen individual investors and large corporations overpay or take heavy losses because the information they were given were not verified. Many investors shy away from the diligence process for two main reasons; they don't want to seem pushy, or they have a phobia for the math and numbers. As it relates to being pushy, it is your money, and there is no need to be a jerk, but there is also no need to be seen as the nicest person on earth.

Remember, you're an angel now—and you are here to help, but you have to be sure that you are helping in the right way. For those with a number's repulsion, a fundamental rule to keep in mind is that the numbers should be simple and easy to understand. It is the business's responsibility to explain them and breakdown how they arrived at a number. If it doesn't make sense, it isn't on you to figure it out.

Others make mistakes in thinking that because they are intelligent, they are experts at everything. Being an expert or being successful in one area of business does not guarantee you success in another. Every industry has its nuisances and norms, especially if the industry is undergoing a paradigm shift. Apply what you know but make sure not to drink your own Kool-Aid.

And some believe that they can just "read" people and tell if something is a good investment. I am a big believer in trusting your gut, but you are not a psychic or a mind reader. I have seen lots of smart people and "instinct" driven people being taken advantage of- a scammer can see you coming from a mile away.

It is therefore necessary to have a strong diligence protocol in place, and it is easy to create one and replicate the process every time you need to investigate a business, you're looking to invest in.In this chapter, we will break down the process into small bits.

A key factor to keep in mind is that you are not going to conduct a deep dive due diligence on every opportunity. You only need to do this with businesses that you are excited about.

If you are indifferent, or just mildly interested in hearing more, it is not worth your time.

Also, avoid initiating a diligence process if you are not serious about writing a check. It is not fair to the businesses, and you do not want to gain a reputation as a person who is just kicking the tires. Word will spread fast and people may start finding it hard to take you seriously.

Let's get ready to take the deep dive.

Proceed With Caution:

How To Vet A Business Idea

In your search for viable businesses to invest in, you'll likely find a lot of businesses that seem like they may need some financial help or need saving but before you even begin to consider investing in any business, you have to first vet the business and if it's a startup, you have to vet the idea.

This helps you sieve the wheat from the chaff and ensure that you are giving your money to people who have similar interests- people who are looking to grow their businesses and make a difference in the community not just people looking to cash out, or people who may end up wasting your money.

One tool that Angel investors and Venture Capitalists use to sieve the wheat from the chaff is the **Business Plan**. In this day and age, every serious entrepreneur should have a business plan. There is a common saying that until you write something down, it's only a wish.

It only becomes a plan after you have written it down.

A business plan is a document that outlines the goals of a business, and how it plans to achieve those goals. Business ideas are a dime a dozen- anyone can dream up ideas but turning ideas into profit requires a plan.

During your search, you'll come across a lot of sweet-talking entrepreneurs with tall dreams and no concrete strategies for achieving those dreams. Like I said earlier, you're not Santa Claus- you're looking to make money while impacting your community, and that means that you cannot afford to put your money in places where it won't make a difference.

This is why you must always, always ask for a business plan whether the business is a small mom-and-pop corner shop, or a startup. Every business should have that simple document that clearly details:

- Who they are
- What they do
- Where they've been
- Where they are going
- Why they need more money
- How they plan to spend it

Basically, the business plan should detail how the money you give them will make a difference or help them reach their goals.

A business plan can be one of the earliest ways to tell a viable investment from a disaster waiting to happen. After meeting with a business owner and establishing that they are open to the idea of an angel investor, ask them for a business plan and study it carefully before you decide to go further with them.

The business plan doesn't have to be formal or be in the standard format because many small business owners may not know how to prepare one and may not be able to afford the services of an expert but there are a few standard questions that every business plan should be able to provide answers to, and every serious entrepreneur should have these answers in their head.

For business owners who are unable to prepare a standard business plan, you can arrange a meeting with them, ask them the necessary questions, and help them write it down.

A business plan should be able to answer the following questions:

- **What is Your Basic Business Concept?** This is where you learn what the business is truly about- the product or services they offer, business locations, and other basic introductory information about the business.
- **What is Your Goal?** This is almost the same the same thing as asking a potential employee the "*Where do you see yourself in the next 10 years*" question in order to see if they fit into your company.

Remember, you're looking to invest in businesses with sustainable growth and development plans for the future, businesses that can be passed down from one generation to another, not businesses that may collapse within a few years.

- **How Do You Plan to Implement It?** This is another area you want to pay close attention to.

For every goal, the business owner must have a clear and sensible plan to achieve it. Keep in mind that your money is going into those goals, so you have to be sure that the business owner knows what they are doing and isn't just trying to build castles in the air.

- **What Competitive Advantage Do You Have Over Your Competitors?** This is especially important when trying to invest in Main street businesses. Many main street businesses operate in industries that are oversaturated and with low barriers for entry.

If you want to invest in such businesses, you have to be sure that it can stand out from the others, or that they have a trick up its sleeves for gaining competitive advantage over others.

- **Who are Your Target Customers?** If the business is seeking to enter a new market, find out who the customers are to see if any opportunities exist in the market they are looking to enter.
- **How Do You Plan to Reach Them?** This is where you ascertain that the company has concrete plans for reaching its target customers. You want to look at things like distribution channels, marketing, and advertising strategies.
- **Who would be managing the Business?** A business

is only as good as its managers, and when I say managers, I'm talking about the employees too.

In a business, everybody who is involved in the day-to-day operations of the business is also a manager. Every single individual contributes significantly to the success or failure of the business whether it's the security guard manning the doors, the waitresses taking and serving orders, or the manager who plans everything on paper.

You can have all the fancy ideas in the world but if you don't have the right hands and minds to help you implement those ideas, the business may still fail.

So, you want to be sure that the businesses you invest in have capable managers and employees that can help to make the business owner's dream come true.

And if it's a typical sole proprietorship with no employees, study the personality of the owner closely, and be sure that they have what it takes to achieve the goals that they have outlined.

- **How Much Do You Need and How Do You Plan to Spend It**: Every business owner seeking capital investment must have an expense budget detailing the total amount they need, and how they plan to spend it.

This is another tool you can use to gauge the viability of the investment. You'll be able to see what they plan to do with your money, if their plans are necessary or relevant to their goals, and if their sales and earnings projections are sufficient to recoup the expenses and earn you any returns or profits within your planned investment period.

For example, if you are looking to invest for 2 years, you want to be sure that the company is able to company can make enough profits to recoup your investments with interests within 2 years.

If an entrepreneur tells you they need $40,000 for instance, and you are only looking to invest for one year, whereas the company only makes $2000 in monthly profits at the moment and have projected that your investment will help them increase that to $4,000 a month, it means they won't be able to refund your money let alone give you any interests on your investments within one year.

Because even if they handed all of their profits to you (which is very unlikely), it will take at least ten months to recoup your investments before even talking about the interests.

So, these are areas you want to look closely into:

How much does the business need?

How much are they currently making?

What is the minimum length of time it will take them to recoup the money I give them together with interests?

> Can I wait for that long?
>
> You should only consider investing when you have looked into these parameters and you are satisfied with the results.

By requesting a business plan, you are not only protecting your interests, but you are also doing the business owner a favor.

A business plan can serve as a blueprint for growth that the owner can always refer back to in the future. It's like having a GPS installed in your vehicle- you know where you are going, where you don't want to go, and how you can get to your destination without unnecessary detours and distractions.

Also, like the saying goes, two good heads are better than one. While looking at the business plan, you may also be able to come up with valuable insights and ideas that the business owner might not have even thought about.

And even if you don't end up investing with them, they can still gain a lot from the advice you give.

So now, you've seen the business plan and you're interested in investing in the business- what next?

Well, you still have to investigate the business further by doing due diligence.

This is the stage where you tell the business owner to provide documents and proofs to back up everything, they've told you so far.

Before You Dive In

Just like putting the funds together to invest took some building work, the due diligence process is going to require some organizing.

Before you begin your review, you need to pull in a critical team member, an attorney.

Everyone should have a relationship with an attorney, specifically, an attorney that specializes in business transactions.

There are some essential documents or agreements that you will need to have your attorney prepare and review: A non-disclosure agreement, a term-sheet, an agreement, and an exit/ release agreement.

Non-Disclosure Agreement

A Non-disclosure agreement is also known as a confidentiality agreement. This agreement is needed to protect the information that is shared by both parties. As an investor, you want to do everything you can to ensure that the businesses you wish to invest in feels protected with you. You will be asking for lots of sensitive data, and in the black community, money matters are an especially sensitive area. I recommend a two-way or mutual NDA. You may also need to disclose information to the business owner or, you may want your identity as an investor protected. One key clause to pay close attention to is the terms of the agreement. In an initial NDA, you will not need more than 18 months in an agreement. The longer the term, the longer you will be on the hook for maintaining those documents. Choose terms that are suitable for the length of time you are investigating. An extended period can be included in the full investment agreement should you get there.

Term Sheet

This can be a very simple document outlining what you are offering, and what you expect in return.

There are some key components to be included:

- How much you are investing, when, and how.

  Some investors prefer to invest in increments, although this will not be relevant for smaller dollar amounts.

  Be sure to place achievable disbursement dates as the business may be depending on those funds.

- What you expect in return and when.

  If you are expecting interest payments, then be sure to outline when those payments start, and how often they are to be made.

  If you are to receive a percentage of ownership, it is important to outline how that will be paid.

  Are you expecting a set percentage of the monthly/quarterly/annual revenue?

In my experience, it is crucial to hammer these things out in the term sheet rather than wasting time with a full agreement.

An Agreement

This is the full agreement. This has all terms from the term sheet, as well as the legal protections in the event that there is a failure to abide with the agreed-upon terms. This will tell both parties how to solve a problem, and when it's time to pull that trigger.

An Exit/Release

Some investments are for a shorter amount of time. It is important to place something in writing that says your obligation has been fulfilled, and both parties are released from the agreement.

Why Use An Attorney?

In this day and age, there are lots of information on the internet that can give an investor a false sense of security.

Some investors may decide that since there are a lot of legal forms and templates for contractual agreements on the internet, they don't need to hire a lawyer to draft one for them.

But you may expose yourself to a lot of risks when you pull a document off the internet and use it, especially when it has to do with investment contracts and agreements.

There is no such thing as a standard contract- there are details that will be important for different deals, or that will vary from industry to industry.

Some legal platforms offer legal documents at low costs. Semi-customization is always better than pulling a document off the internet, but it's still a risky prospect. Depending on the platform, and the contents of the document, the legal documents may still pose a risk.

Many people shy away from using an attorney due to the fear of the costs; however, attorneys are always less expensive on the front end of a partnership as opposed to when you have to bring them in after the situation has gone bad.

Nonetheless, there are a few cost-saving measures that you can deploy to keep your costs low.

If you do not have a trusted attorney in your life already (or one that is connected to a firm that offers representation in multiple areas), then you can meet with several attorneys and see what their capabilities and hourly rates are.

Be upfront with the attorney and let them know that you are looking for counsel and looking to make the right decision.

Do not string them along or promise your business just to see how they might operate. They are most effective when you are honest.

In the conversation, do pay attention to how the attorney interacts with you. If they make you feel dumb, or you do not understand what they are talking about, or they seem annoyed by questions, then they are not the attorney for you.

Think of your attorney like your priest- you have to be comfortable with them because you will need to tell them everything.

To save attorney costs, you can try one or more of the following methods:

Bundling

Bundling is exactly what it sounds like. Some attorneys offer packages of documents for a set price. They likely have worked with lots of businesses with similar needs, so they have designed go-to packages.

Some attorneys' also offer prepaid hour packages. These packages generally come with some discount on the hourly rate if you prepay for pockets of time.

Not all firms offer these options, but it never hurts to ask.

Review Only

If you are particularly sensitive to pricing, and you are comfortable writing, then you may want to consider writing out your documents and having an attorney review them to ensure they offer adequate protection.

Skip the formalities or trying to sound like an attorney and stick to regular language. Write exactly what you mean.

A simple straight forward agreement will get you significantly farther than trying to be fancy.

Opp

That's right- Other People's Property.

You can save on some costs by requesting to execute the other person's agreement, but I still suggest having an attorney review it so that you know what is in the agreement. Remember, generally, the person who creates the document will make sure that it favors their position. If you decide to use documents provided for you-YOU MUST READ THEM THOROUGHLY!

Start-Up Investing

If you are more interested in investing in startups rather than main street businesses, the need for legal review and representation is heightened as you are much more likely to need to protect the proprietary information of a startup.

The term sheet and ultimately, the agreement or convertible note, will not be a simple two-page agreement. It most likely will be 5+ pages in length. While you can deploy some of the strategies mentioned above, including having an attorney read and review the documents provided to you, it is not recommended that you do this alone.

Having an attorney can be very helpful in negotiations and resolving disputes without going to court. No matter what avenue you decide, do not simply skip putting things in writing. Handshake deals are a terrible deal and usually come back to bite you. Remember, everyone hears conversations differently, so it is essential to get things in writing, so everyone is on the same page.

Chapter Summary/Key Takeaways

In this chapter, we discuss the importance of due diligence and having the proper documentation, and how to go about it without burning a hole in your pocket or exposing yourself to avoidable risks.

An attorney can be critical to protecting you.

However, when just starting out cost savings can be a major consideration hence, we have discussed several options that can reduce your cost burden, but still provide you with the necessary protection.

In the next chapter, we discuss how to move into due diligence: which documents to request, and what to look for.

CHAPTER EIGHT: PROVE IT!

As we discussed previously, the due diligence process is that part of the investment process where you are telling the business to prove that what they are saying is true.

You should always verify everything, especially those details that are most crucial to your decision making.

Before you begin requesting information, be sure to sign a non-disclosure agreement first.

The Laundry List

Each section outlines documents to request. In each section, there will be documents that are non-negotiable and a necessity, and some that may not be necessary depending on the stage of development the business is currently in, or the industry in which they operate.

Corporate Documents

1. **Articles of Incorporation**- The articles of incorporation are a must-have document whether the business is a startup or a main street business.

This document tells you that the business is registered with the Secretary of State.

If you are looking into a main street business or a startup with a brick-and-mortar location, then the business should be incorporated in the state where the site is or be appropriately registered as an out of state entity that has permission to operate in the state.

If the business is a startup that is tech-based or tech-enabled, then the company's articles of incorporation may be in another state.

Delaware, for instance, is a popular state of incorporation.

Even if the company provides you with a PDF file of the articles of incorporation, be sure to go to the website of the secretary of state for that state and look up the entity.

Be sure that the company is still current in the database.

Also, verify who the registered owner of the business truly is just to be sure that you are negotiating with the right person.

In main street businesses, it is not uncommon for a parent to be the actual owner of a business, and the children to have taken over.

However, if you see that the business changes owners frequently or the company has been administratively dissolved, you should make a note, and ask follow-up questions. Frequent owner changes could signal financial or legal issues, and administrative dissolution may be revealing some documentation deficits that should be explored.

The business will need to be properly registered before you move forward with the investment.

Depending on the industry, there may be other registration requirements.

2. **Bylaws, Operating, Partnership Agreements**- An operating agreement, and/or bylaws, should be present if you are considering a startup.

Main street businesses may not have taken this step, especially if there is only one owner.

The operating/ partnership agreements include the rules of the business functioning. If there are multiple members of the company, how decisions, including investment decisions are to be made, are spelt out in the operating/partnership agreements.

It's always good to know who has the final say in the company, and to familiarize yourself with what your potential role may be as outlined in the document.

3. **Certificates from All States and Jurisdictions where the Company Does Business**- This is similar to the articles of incorporation.

Every state that the business operates in should be appropriately accounted for and documented.

4. ***Other Ownership Agreements****- Request any other agreements that grant ownership stakes to others.*

For a main street business, this could be another investor, and for a startup, this could be other outstanding convertible notes.

If they do exist, you will need to factor that into your decision.

First, do some quick math. Be sure to make that the ownership stake being offered is available.

I have seen cash strapped owners offer portions of their business to multiple people and end up giving away more than 100%.

If the startup has other outstanding convertible notes, pay close attention to the amount of interest that they are currently paying.

Convertible notes are a great option, but they can saddle a startup with burdensome payments early in their revenue-generating life.

Financial Information

The financial information should be a core focus of your diligence. Every business should have a handle on their finances if they are a viable investment prospect. Having a handle on your finances means knowing how much money you bring in each month, and how much you spend. The business should have some established system for tracking this information.

For established businesses, this may be a point-of-sale system tracking the register or credit card systems. Cash-only businesses are a bit harder to verify. For this reason, investing in a cash-only business may be risky.

Startups that are pre-revenue may have limited financials. They are more likely to have forecasts but not sales records.

1. **Official Financial Statements**- For main street businesses, this will likely be tax returns.

It is important to request several years, 3-5 years.

It is important to look for trends: Are the sales growing or are they flat? Does the business show a profit?

Be sure to compare the tax returns to any internal accounting documents. If you see discrepancies between what is reported to the IRS, and what the owner says to you, this is a red flag.

The last thing you want is the IRS coming into the picture and auditing the business that you just took a stake in.

While it is positive for the company have a professional independently preparing the financials, do not penalize the company if they don't, especially if the books are in good order.

2. **Budget**- The business should have a profit and loss statement.

They may not call it a P&L, but the business should know what it brings in, and what it spends. This is not negotiable.

3. **Financial Projections**-Financial projections are a

must for a startup.

A poorly kept secret is that in general, financial projections are not very reliable.

The projections for a startup should be for five years but pay more attention to the projections for years 1 to 3.

Projections are based on assumptions or the startup's best hypothesis on what will happen. These assumptions should be clear.

They include how many customers they will sell to each year, how much they will charge, how much the product or service will cost the business, employee salaries, etcetera.

Pay close attention to a few key factors. If the sales go from 0 to 1 million in the first year, the projections are likely worthless. Sales take time to develop, so it is unlikely that a 7-figure business will emerge in year one.

Pay attention to how many employees, especially sales employees. A mistake several new startups make is projecting sales with no employees.

A single founder will be wearing a lot of hats, and if they are the only person driving sales, their sales are likely to fall short of their projections.

Finally, look at the profit margin, including taxes. Most startups do not turn a profit in the first few years. If the company is projecting a profit, take a look at whether they have accounted for taxes. If they have not, then it is likely that they missed other costs. It is vital to question the projections but do keep in mind that this is an area most entrepreneurs get wrong. Use your own analysis to adjust the projections.

4. **Current Business Plan**- Every business should have some sort of plan for the future.

If the business is a main street, this is likely to be much less formal. Often, an owner will have the plan in their head. If this is the case, you need to listen carefully and document the plan in a quick and easy way. If they have been looking to expand offerings, or do renovations, they should have some costs that correspond to their plans.

All startups should have a more formalized business plan. Expect these plans to include robust sales and marketing strategy, and a technology or platform development plan. Competitive intelligence, complete financials, and market data should be thorough.

5. **Accounts Receivable and Accounts Payable**- This only applies to the established main street businesses and startups that are generating revenue.

Accounts receivable are the amounts owed to a company by its customers, while accounts payable are the amounts that a company owes to its suppliers. Be sure to pay close attention to both line items. If there are a lot of accounts receivable dollars that have been outstanding for greater than 90 days, that is a potential red flag that the company is carrying significant bad debt. In other words, they are making sales, but the customers are not paying on time. If there are lots of payable dollars outstanding, that could indicate cash flow problems or possibly bad credit with suppliers.

The business should also disclose if it has write-offs/bad debt.

6. **Product or Service Pricing Plans and Policies**-No matter the type of business it is, there should be defined pricing.

This may or may not be a stand-alone document. When evaluating the pricing structure, think about it from the perspective of a customer. Make sure that the pricing makes sense for the customer base. If the company is a startup, there should be some data (a survey, industry trends, or competitor pricing) that gives some guidance.

7. **Contracts and Agreements**- All agreements or contracts should be in writing.

If there are large (major corporate) agreements, it is important to review those documents. Specifically, you should figure out how long is left on the contract and verify that they are in good standing. If there is a new contract, like a new government contract for example, be sure that you understand what is needed to secure the contract fully, and when the first payments will come in.

Be careful with "partnerships" that do not yield actual revenue. While some partnership can boost credibility, investigate and determine whether that increase in credibility has yielded any results. If there is no documentation of the agreement, do not use it as a factor for investment.

8. **Who They Owe**- If the company owes anyone money, be sure to know the necessary details.

You should know how much is owed, what the monthly payments are, and whether the company is current or in default. Be sure to ask about liens, equipment leases, mortgages, or any other outstanding loans or debt that reduces the company profit.

Compliance

This will vary significantly from business to business. One common compliance document is business insurance. Every business has risks, and insurance helps to reduce that risk should things go wrong. Certain industries require specific limits, so be sure that the business is in compliance. All permits and licenses should be verified to be current and in good standing.

Litigation

Conduct a public record - check to be sure that no legal cases are outstanding. If your search finds a case, then fully understand the status, including potential damages. Search for any other claims or public filings like bankruptcy or liens on any property. If any cases have been settled, be sure that it has been properly documented, and the business has fulfilled its part of the bargain.

Management And Personnel

For main street businesses, the employees who manage and interact with customers are critical. Don't be surprised if the owner has hired several family members. This can be both a blessing and a curse. Hiring family can mean increased loyalty, but it can also mean lax enforcement of business rules and procedures. Observe family dynamics in the business settings to understand the potential risks.

If the company is a startup, the management should be a particular focus. If the startup has only one team member-the founder, that is a potential red flag. Everyone needs a team. Understand the background of the founder. Do they have industry experience? If the answer is no, then the need for a team is of greater importance.

Do not mistake education for experience. Education does confer some knowledge, but it is not a substitute for hands-on experience. Both are important but don't count a business owner or founder out because they do not have a formal education.

Pay close attention to the organizational management chart and bios of senior personnel. Even the savviest investors place great importance on the quality of the management team.

Intellectual Property

This will not apply to all companies or startups. Intellectual property includes Patents, trademarks, and trade secrets. Having intellectual property can give a competitive advantage. If the company has a recognizable brand, a trademark is important. If the company has trade secrets, these should remain secret. These will not and should not be disclosed to you. Trade secrets only keep their value if few people know it.

Finally, patents are great but very expensive to secure and maintain, and typically take years to acquire. Some terms to listen for are patent-pending, filed, granted, and abandoned. A filed patent means just that. It means that the paperwork is on record at the patent office. Patent-pending means that the patent is moving through the system. An abandoned patent means that the process was started, but the business did not follow it through.

It is important to note that even though abandoned patents can be revived, the process is not as simple as filing again on the same product.

Granted patents are the most valuable. These give the most protection. However, pay attention to how much time is left before it expires. Twenty years is the usual term of a patent and having much time left is very important.

Also, note that intellectual property is a very complex field. If the founder or owner filed the application, it might have a more difficult time getting through.

Use Of Funds

Simply put, this is how the business intends to use your investment. This should be clear, with the numbers well defined.

Large buckets like working capital or sales growth are not sufficient. Those are headers- there should be more details on the line items.

The costs should also be verifiable. While the funds may be coming in the nick of time, make sure that they are enough to weather the storm. If the funds only help for a month or two before the business is back in a rut, then this may not be a wise investment.

Two final keys to diligence are the interview, and the visit(s). You should have extended conversations with the owners.

You should never refer to the interactions as interviews, but you will use them as assessments, much like a job interview, to gain insights into the owner's mindset and personality.

Visit or patronize the business several times. If there is a physical brick and mortar establishment, allow the owners to give you a formal tour and after that, visit the business unannounced a few different times.

You should observe the business when customer traffic is high, and when it is at the lowest.

If the target is a startup, then go through the business' process.

If it is a service, go through the process as an unannounced or secret shopper. But first, have a good understanding of how the founder has described the process before you visit. Your secret shopper experience should give you an insight into what other customers are receiving.

In both of these scenarios, be sure that you are not receiving any preferential treatment. It may be necessary to send an associate so that you are not recognized.

Chapter Summary/Key Takeaways

Remember that the diligence process is your opportunity to verify all that has been presented to you. No company is perfect, and there may be gaps in the documentation. Do not be shy when requesting documents. If the owner or the founder is irritated with the requests for documentation, walk away. The diligence process is not intended to cause embarrassment or harm. Pay close attention to whether the documents match the narrative. Trust is a key component of any investment. If the owner is continuously correcting the record or has complicated explanations, this is not a positive sign and should not be ignored. Careful investigation on the front end of any investment will save you pain, time, and money.

In the next chapter, you will learn about setting expectations and how to evaluate the opportunity and all of the documents as a whole.

CHAPTER NINE: KNOWING WHEN

In the previous chapter, we discuss documents to request when considering investing. Unless you have been an attorney, or in a finance position, you may be saying great, I have all of this information, now what? How do I move through these documents, and make sense of them?

There are plenty of resources that can teach you how to read a profit and loss statement or how to make sense of a marketing strategy, but I will instead walk you through scenarios.

Like Kenny Rogers famously wrote: *...You've got to know when to hold'em, know when to fold'em, know when to walk away, and know when to run...*

Like the gambler, an investor has to know when to go all the way in, and when to run away.

Know When to Hold 'Em

These are your best-case scenarios- the opportunities to hold on to and make an investment.

Scenario 1

In this scenario, the company has all of its documents in good order and is current.

This is not a likely scenario as angel investors are needed by those who are bootstrapping their way through and in need of some assistance.

If you are looking for a business that has all green lights and no red flags, then you will likely never invest a single dollar.

Scenario 2

The Shiny Parts:

- You have met with the owners of the business and have a rapport. They are open to your ideas, and you are comfortable with their vision of how to grow.
- The owners are financially vested in the business. This means the business should be the primary source of income of its owner.

As a first-time investor, you want to be sure that the owner will take the wins and losses with you.

- The business has been in the area for more than five years, is seen as a staple, and enjoys a good reputation.
- The business is properly registered, and all insurance and business permits are in place.
- The business is generating revenue and clears at least a small profit.
- The business is not carrying any substantial debt and has not defaulted on their loan obligations. The business may have a mortgage, but it is current, and there are no second or third mortgages.

The Warts:

- The business's profit is minimal—they may have thin margins for their industry, or the slim profit margins may be due to poor purchasing power, incorrect pricing, or top-heavy human resource burdens.
- The business has some amount of "downtime" or low customer traffic a few days of the week.
- The building/facility could use some improvements- either aesthetic or structural.
- Little to no marketing outside of word of mouth or local legend.

A company in this scenario may make a good investment as this company has good financial health.

All of the warts mentioned above are all areas where your capital can be used to make a difference.

The most attractive of all the shiny parts (in addition to being profitable), is the owner's coachability. This serves as a foundation for a good investment relationship.

This scenario is more likely to be a main street business because very few early-stage startups are likely to be generating any revenue or profit.

Know When To Fold 'Em

The scenarios in this category cover those investments that are going to require a bit of work before you are all in.

Scenario 1

The Shiny Parts:

- The owners have a clear vision of how to grow the business.
- The owners may be financially vested in the business. This could be a second or third business, so they have some sort of business track record.
- The business owner enjoys a good reputation or has credibility in the industry and/or in the community.
- The business is properly registered, and all insurance and business permits are in place.
- The business is generating revenue.
- The business is carrying some debt, and the debt may be eating profit margin, but they are current on all debt obligations.

The Warts:

- The business has no profit— while the business is making money, the overhead is destroying the margins.
- There is a significant amount of operational inefficiency.
- The business has a large amount of "downtime" or low customer traffic throughout the week. There may be only one or two days that actually support the business.
- The building/facility could use some improvements- either aesthetic or structural.
- Little to no marketing outside of word of mouth, or local legend.

Scenario 2

The Shiny Parts

- The owner wants to grow but does not have a defined vision for how that will happen.
- The business has been in the area for more than one year and is on an upswing for customer traffic and growth.
- The business is properly registered, and all insurance and business permits are in place.
- The business is generating some revenue but is currently operating at a loss.

The Warts:

- The business is carrying substantial debt but is current.
- The business is operating at a loss due to the debt burden or overhead.
- Poor foot traffic due to the young age of the business.
- The building/facility is newer but not owned.
- There is some marketing, but it is still too soon to tell if it is effective and will generate repeat business.

The investments in this category may still be a quality one, but it will require a bit more of a hands-on approach.

You will need to help develop a plan and strategy, and you may also need to help out with the execution.

If these are not your strong suits, always use the Hippocratic Oath approach—first, do no harm.

You want to come in as a help, not another burden.

In these scenarios, if you will have to contribute your talent and expertise in a significant way, you can negotiate a higher ownership stake.

Know When To Walk Away

Companies that find themselves in this category are not ready for investment at the current time. This happens quite often. Many businesses think that what they lack is capital. But often, inadequate capital is only part of the problem. However, this may be no fault of the business owner.

When a business is in the bootstrap mode for an extended period, there may not have been a lot of resources to dedicate to efficiency and process optimization.

This could mean that administrative filings have fallen through the cracks, or that there are more manual processes that are more subject to human area.

Scenario 1

The Shiny Parts:

- The owners are working hard on the business.
- The business is generating revenue (even if uneven).

The Warts:

- The business has some state or local registration or certification issues.
- The business has a poor understanding of how they make money.
- The business has a poor understanding of how much money they are making.
- The business is understaffed, or the owner is the only worker.
- There is a significant amount of operational inefficiency.
- Revenue is very unpredictable or sporadic.

Scenario 2

The Shiny Parts:

- The business is already in existence.

The Warts:

- The business has some state or local registration or certification issues.
- The business is not generating revenue.
- The business is winging it—or they have little to no operational protocol.
- The business is open, yet there is little name recognition or consumer base.

The investments in this category have the potential to be good businesses; however, it is still too soon to tell.

They have some basic business operations issues to work out before pulling in an investor.

There may be an opportunity to come on board as a co-founder or co-owner, but that will likely require a more significant investment of both time and money.

Do not fall for the allure of putting in a small amount of capital in exchange for a large percentage of the business. You are likely to own a large portion of something that yields a negative return and delivers significant headaches.

Know When To Run Away

The Shiny Parts:

- There are no apparent bright spots after further investigation.

The Warts:

- The business is not registered or has been ordered to close due to violations.
- Initial information provided does not match the documentation that was provided.
- The business or the owner does not have a good reputation in the community they are looking to serve.
- The business or the owner has outstanding judgments, litigation or IRS debt.

While this might seem like a no-brainer, many investors fall for the diamond in the rough or the savior narrative.

The diamond in the rough and savior narratives will make you ignore actual red flags and try to resurrect the business or the owner.

Reviving even a small business is a tough feat.

Remember, you are not a charity, and you aren't resurrecting companies from the dead. You are an investor, and there needs to be a clear path to your making money.

Chapter Summary/Key Takeaways

In this chapter, rather than providing a how-to on reviewing financial statements, we move through real-world scenarios.

In businesses that are ready for investment, the good will significantly outweigh the bad. if this not the case, then take it as an indicator that the business is not completely ready for investment.

CHAPTER TEN: SETTING EXPECTATIONS

Setting expectations throughout the entire process is critical to keeping all parties on the same page. It will reduce headaches and save you from miscommunication.

Money Due Date

The first expectation that should be set is when the business will need the investment. The reply from the business will be very telling.

If the business needs the funding with 30 days, this is a red flag and this may not the business that you invest in.

However, some investors may want to meet an urgent/emergent need. If this is the case, you should only make that kind of emergency leap with someone that you have an established relationship with.

One reason is that the timeframe does not leave you with much time to verify information independently, and that is a problem.

In these cases, the funding is less likely to be fueling growth and is more of a bailout.

In rare cases, it is for gap funding for an event or promotion, but you still need to take time to investigate. So, what should be your investment timeline?

I suggest 45-90 days, depending on the complexity of the investment.

This period should allow you time to conduct all of the interviews, visits, and data verification necessary. It also gives you time to move funds if needed.

Keep in mind that if you can complete your process sooner, and you are satisfied that you are well informed about the business and all its intricacies, then you are free to make the investment.

Easy Does It

DO NOT FEEL PRESSURED!

Businesses can make you feel like you have to move now. You both need each other, but high-pressure tactics are not a good sign. It could be revealing that the money is more desperately needed than originally presented. A common approach is the

FOMO or fear of missing out talk line. This can look like "act now because I only allow a few people in" or, we have a line of investors throwing money at us. If things are moving too fast, just pass on the opportunity.

What You Really Want

Be upfront with what you want in return, and why you want to invest. Do not feel the need to over-explain yourself or create some grandiose long-term vision.

It is completely acceptable to say- I saw this as a good investment opportunity, and I think I can make a return on my money. If you are in this to make money, be comfortable with that. It can be difficult in some communities to be upfront and vocal about your desire to prosper financially, but this does not make you a predator, and you should turn a deaf ear to anyone who speaks of your efforts in this way.

If you want to be an active part of the business, then it is vital to be clear about what that means.

Does that mean you will be coming by every day?

Does it mean you want to have a look at the books on a set interval?

Does it mean you want to help with the strategy and execution behind the scenes?

Conversely, do you wish to remain unbothered and simply receive the agreed-upon payments?

Communicating this directly is important.

Length Of Time

The next expectation that needs to be set is how long you want to be an investor. This will be dependent on your risk tolerance, industry, and personality. If you are just looking to get your feet wet, then a shorter term may be more suitable. If you are investing in a start-up, this is likely going to be a longer timeframe likely to be higher than three years.

When deciding how long you want to stay in, consider whether you are expecting a large return or something more marginal.

If you are looking to double your money in a year, that is not a realistic expectation.

Longer investment horizons offer a more significant opportunity for more substantial returns. This does not mean that if you invest longer, then you will always make more.

Furthermore, it would be best if you gave whatever improvements that were made to the business time to work.

Unless you are offering working capital for a product or inventory that already has purchase orders, you will have to invest for longer than six months.

I suggest a 12-15-month initial term for main street investments and 2-4 years for venture investments.

This will give you time to look at the trend, and an option to pull all of your money out without a penalty.

While these expectations may be slightly tweaked depending on the particular circumstances, be firm in what you expect.

There are very few right or wrong answers when it comes to your expectations, be sure to stick to your guns, and find the opportunity that best suits you.

Return

The final expectation to set prior and evaluate is the amount of return that you want.

The average check written by individual angel investors is a little more than $36,000, and the median is $25,000. However, there is a broad range of check sizes, from $5,000 to $100,000 (Hudson, 2017).

The report also shows differences in investment sizes by region, length of time investing, by background, and by gender.

Since 1923, the average return in the stock market (S&P 500) has been 12% (Reuters, 2013).

Angel investors experience higher returns, but they are not quick turnarounds.

Angel investing can be risky business. Most prior studies posit that 5-10 percent of investments will be economically profitable. In the American Angel, investors said on average, 11 percent of their total portfolio yielded a positive exit.

A study conducted in 2014 about angel investors by the Ewing Marion Kauffman Foundation, and the Angel Capital Education Foundation, found that angel investor exits generated 2.6 times the invested capital in 3.5 years from investment to exit.

This study highlights two key observations:

1- The rate of return can be higher on angel investments.

2- 2- These investments are longer-term investments.

Based on this let's do some quick math—

A $10,000 investment would yield $26,000 over 3.5 years or just over $7,400 per year ($619/mo.)—Not a bad return.

All evidence suggests that angel investors can expect approximately 2.5X return over time.

So, when thinking about how much return to expect, 2.5X is an excellent place to start.

Keep in mind that if you want to pull out of an investment earlier than the 2-3-year mark, you will need to consider a lower multiple.

The 2.5X return should act as a guide when looking at the projections.

In the next section, we will discuss the deal structure as the structure of the deal will have a direct impact on your returns.

Chapter Summary/Key Takeaways

In this chapter, we discuss setting your expectations. Upfront and decisive is the name of the game. If there is too much ambiguity, then you will likely not have an optimal experience. If you find it challenging to decide exactly where you stand, give yourself time. You are in no rush to invest. When in doubt, circle back to your financial audit and examine what your return goals might be, and that might point you in the right direction.

PART IV: THE DEAL

"You must never try to make all the money that's in a deal. Let the other fellow make some money too, because if you have a reputation for always making all the money, you won't have many deals."

– J. Paul Getty

CHAPTER ELEVEN: LET'S MAKE A DEAL

One of the fundamental principles of investing is low risk = low reward, and high risk = high reward. Identifying risk can be tough. Even more challenging is how to determine what the probability that an owner or founder will be successful is.

This is where investing in what you know is particularly helpful because as much as we can apply logic or math to investment, the more you know, the quicker your gut instincts will kick in, and help guide you through decision making.

In chapter six, we moved through several scenarios. These scenarios were ranked from the best case to the worst-case scenarios.

The risk would correlate with those scenarios.

The "hold 'em" scenarios correspond to low risk, while the "runaway" scenarios are the highest risk. Therefore, an existing business with steady revenue that is looking to grow has less risk than a startup venture with no income at all.

If you have moved through the diligence process in a careful, thoughtful manner, then you are in complete control of the strength and weaknesses of the business.

In this chapter, we will discuss how to structure your deal to increase your return, and how to reduce your risks.

Debt Versus Equity

When speaking in terms of investment, most people automatically think that what they receive in return is an ownership stake or equity.

Instead of crafting your deal for equity, you may want to consider setting it up like a debt, in other words, like a loan.

All states have established guidelines for loans, including providing ways to secure it.

Most people are familiar with collateral and how that can be used in a loan.

In many cases, you file a document called a Universal Code 1 (UCC-1). By filling this document, you as an investor moves from a general creditor to a secured creditor.

This filing says that you (the investor) have an interest in the specified property.

This structure could be especially valuable for main street investments.

Similarly, rather than just taking equity in an early-stage company, a convertible note allows for repayment, and warrants allow you an option to buy common stock for next to nothing in the future should they be worth something.

In an early investment, this could be very valuable because as an angel investor, you are putting some of the first money in. This is in hopes that you help the company move to the next stage and attract a larger check to help them on the way.

In this scenario, exercising your warrant may mean getting an even larger reward for taking the early risk.

Terms

After deciding on whether you wish to make your investment more like a debt, or choose to go with equity, you need to present the terms to the business.

This can be done in several forms: verbally, via a term sheet, or a commitment letter.

In most instances, I don't advise the terms to be presented verbally. Putting terms in writing is critical.

A term sheet is a one-page document that outlines the deal. This document should spell out the high level (and important) details.

A commitment letter has significantly more details.

I recommend a term sheet for the simple deals, small investments and main street investments, and the commitment letter for startup investments that will be for a longer period, especially those opportunities that you believe will be high growth (high return) investments.

A term sheet should have the following details:

- **The business**: In this section, you should be detailing the business and the proprietary products of value.

Define this very carefully as you do not wish to have the business make significant changes before the investment is made.

- **Consideration**: This is where you identify what you are giving (money/expertise/network), and what you are getting (equity, monthly payments, board seat).

This section can also include additional requirements like allowing control of customer lists or securing the supply chain.

- **Purchase Price**: This could be the price that you are acquiring shares for, or the amount that will be invested in the business.
- **Payment Terms**: Simply put, how do you plan to get your money back?

This is where you define any interests, due payment dates, payment intervals, when the payments should begin, and when they should end.

This section should be as detailed as possible.

- **Due Diligence**: Yes, you have already conducted diligence, but after presenting a term sheet, you may want to forward certain documents or agreements to a financial advisor and maybe your attorney for review.

The diligence period after a term sheet is presented a bit more defined. In real estate, this could be anywhere from 30-180 days, depending on the complexity of the work that needs to be completed.

In most cases, this second phase of diligence is less than 45 days.

Be sure to check with all the people who will be conducting reviews on your behalf to be sure that they can complete the work within the set time frame.

A savvy business owner may require that you pay a penalty if you back out as compensation for the loss of time or the effort put in.

A key provision in this section is that the information has to be acceptable to the expert.

This means while you may have done an initial review, a professional may offer a different opinion which could mean that you can back out based on those findings.

- **Closing Conditions**: These terms include provisions like:

-The information will remain valid on the closing date.

-That the owner is properly following all laws and provisions.

-That you, the investor, has procured or has made arrangements for funds to be available to close the deal.

-The owner has the authority to complete the transaction.

-The investor is satisfied with the due diligence findings.

- **Governing Law**: This defines the court where any disputes will be resolved.

In most cases, as the investor, you should choose the state that is most convenient for you. In some exceptional cases, you may be choosing a state that has the most business-friendly laws.

Your attorney can give you the best guidance on where you should select.

If necessary, you may need to state that business will be conducted in the English language.

- **Fees and Expenses**: If there are costs associated with completing the deal, then it is recommended that each side covers its expenses.

For business owners, this keeps costs down, and for investors, this helps in being decisive.

Paralysis by analysis can be a real thing, so capping your expenditures is wise.

- **Binding or Non-binding Terms**: Term sheets can come in two varieties: binding and non-binding.

A binding term sheet means that each part is held to this agreement.

Furthermore, barring a limited set of circumstances, the deal will go through.

A binding term sheet holds more weight than a non-binding version. However, there are reasons why a non-binding term sheet should be presented.

If there is significant diligence left to do, or if the deal is contingent on other factors or conditions being met, a non-binding term sheet can give both sides more opportunity to walk away.

If the term sheet is binding, the term sheet should prohibit the business from conducting any other ownership stakes or making other transactions that might change the return profile.

- **Confidentiality**: Yes, this is in addition to the NDA (Non-Disclosure Agreement) that you signed previously.

This section requires that each side agrees that this term sheet is for a potential transaction between the investor and the owner and is confidential.

This includes both the specific terms, including investment amount, and return or interest.

In some cases, it may be wise to keep confidential that the deal is being negotiated or considered.

- **Expiration Date**: Any terms offered should expire.

  This helps not to waste either side's time. Most term sheets are only valid for 14-30 days after the stated diligence period is over.

Term sheets are negotiable. Be sure to give the business time to review the terms.

The terms that are set in the term sheet should have an expiration date. That date should give the business enough time to consider the terms properly.

While there is no need to rush, 14 days is generally enough time for review.

The business may want to amend some of the terms. Any amendments have to make sense and be aligned with the goals and expectations that were set.

Two popular terms that the business may fight to have amended are the amount of capital to be invested and the ownership stake.

While these are popular negotiation points, they are linked together. The relationship between the investment amount and the ownership stake is determined in most terms by the business valuation.

However, valuations can be very tricky.

For startups that do not have previous capital invested or revenue generation, valuations may not hold much value.

Many startups will come with their own valuation numbers. If you are the first money in, it is a better idea to invest your funds via a convertible note. This will allow you to convert to an ownership stake at a later date when a proper valuation can be reached.

For main street businesses, a valuation can be reached using several methods.

An effortless way to find the value of a business is through business insurance. Depending on the type of policy, a valuation for the business may have been reached for insurance purposes. This may overvalue the business, but it could be a starting point.

Understanding Business Valuations

Method 1: Asset-Based

The asset-based method evaluates the business's assets and liabilities.

To calculate the value of the business, you have to find the difference between assets and liabilities.

When you use the asset-based method, you look at your business as being made up of smaller parts. Some parts add value to your company. Other parts add debts to your business.

Items that add value are assets, while liabilities are the debts your company owes to creditors.

There are some pros and cons to this method.

This method is popular for asset-heavy businesses-those businesses that own property or pieces of equipment.

If the business owns the property outright, and there are no other outstanding lenders or liens, this methodology could be beneficial.

If the equipment is being leased, this method is not very useful as the value of the asset will be offset by the debt it carries.

Also, many main street businesses may find themselves in an asset poor situation.

The asset method is similar to how a bank would decide if a business were eligible for a loan. The assets would be likely termed the collateral.

If you use this method to value the business, you may want to consider tying your investment to those assets for security.

To determine the value of the business, subtract liabilities from the assets.

Here's a general example, if the business has $100,000 in assets and $30,000 in liabilities, the value of the business is $70,000 ($100,000 – $30,000 = $70,000).

A con to this method is determining the value of the assets (the liabilities are easy; bills and payments help you determine this quickly). The challenge with finding the value of equipment or property often lies with finding the book value.

However, the asset-based method could be beneficial if the business needs to be sold quickly, or if you are looking to invest enough in the business to control a significant stake.

If the owner of a business is relying heavily on this method, the business may not be very healthy. This method generally keeps the value low which could be good for the investor but keep in mind that there may be some significant warts that warrant a fast sell and not much price haggling.

Method 2: Market

The method will be familiar if you have ever purchased a home.

The "comparables" of houses in the area are often pulled to help verify and validate the value of the home to be purchased.

The market method compares your business to similar companies that have already been sold.

Here is a simple example:

Let's say the business you are looking to invest in is a salon, and other salons in the area are selling for an average of $60,000. Using the market method, the business is worth about $60,000.

The market method offers an amount close to the fair market value.

Finding "true" comparable businesses may be challenging. A proper comparable business should be of similar size, revenue generation, and possibly even geographical location. The more factors that match, the more relevant the valuation will be.

This type of data in a general public search is hard to come by. Most of the data that can be easily found will be of public companies which from a size and scope perspective are not relevant even if the industry is the same; a McDonald's is not the same as a local family burger spot.

There is a general business principle that a target is only worth what someone is willing to pay for it. This can cut both ways for an investor. If there is another investor or offer on the table, and the other investor is willing to pay more, then by default, the business is worth more- the competition drives up the price.

If you are the only investor, then what you are willing to pay sets the price.

While this can be exciting, be fair and reasonable as you are looking to be an angel investor, not a vulture.

The value of the business depends on the market. This can pose an issue if the market the business is in is shrinking, or the economy is down.

If this is the case, this can depress the value; this may be a good thing for an investor as the dollars invested will buy more of the business.

Method 3: Income

The income method is what I recommend. The income method looks at the business's financial history and financial health.

Using all of the financial documents that you requested and gathered during due diligence, you can evaluate the business's financial health.

With the income method, you look at the businesses past profit, revenue, and cash flow using your profit and loss statement, or previous tax returns.

Use at least three years if available and pay close attention to the trend.

Notice if the revenue line is going up every year, staying the same, decreasing, or all over the place.

Then take a look at the profit (the line that says "*after all expenses were taken out*"). Look at the same trends. Evaluate if the two lines show the same trends.

If the revenue is going up, and the profit is going down, that could be a sign that the increase in sales costs more to achieve.

If the revenue is going down or staying steady and the profit trend is going up, then this could be a sign that the business is becoming more efficient.

By examining the previous years and looking at the trends, especially the percent growth year over year, then you can project what the revenue and profits may be for the next few years during your investment.

If the company has only been in business for a year or less, then you can use the month over month revenue and profits. However, use the month over month number to project months, not several years as it could be misleading.

With this method, the value of the business is the amount of money the business makes.

When making an offer for the business, your price will likely be the average revenue or profit number per year, multiplied by the number of years the owner is charging.

Quick Math

If the average revenue per year equals $250,000, an offer of $1.25M would be paying for the "revenue lost" to the owner for 5 years.

A Quick Note on Revenue, Earnings, Receipts, Profit

As previously discussed, top-line revenue in a company's financial statements is the money received before a product or service. It is also called receipts.

Bottom line revenue, on the other hand, is the number that is left after all the costs of running the company, and making the product, including taxes are deducted. This is also known as profit.

There is another common line used for valuation, and that is the EBIT and EBITDA line.

EBIT is earnings before interest and taxes, while EBITDA is Earnings before interest, taxes, depreciation, and amortization.

Sometimes, the earnings are adjusted to take out income taxes, non-recurring income and expenses, non-operating income and expenses, depreciation and amortization, interest expense or interest income, or owner compensation.

Method 4: Valuing A Business With Multiples Of Earnings

In most cases, EBIT (earnings before interest and taxes) is the measure used for the earnings number.

Similar to the previous approach, multiple is used to determine the value.

The "multiple" is the number you multiply the baseline number by.

The market or an industry peer determines the multiple. There are some national standards, depending on industry type and business size.

The multiple can be positive or negative. A negative multiple would be appropriate if there are significant negative factors present. This would result in the valuation of the company being less than one.

Let's say the multiple is two. If the earnings of the business are $900,000, the multiples of earnings calculation mean the business may be valued for sale at $1,800,000.

Keep in mind that according to Bizbuysell, the average business sells for around 0.6 times its annual revenue, nationally.

Think of the average or profit revenue line as the baseline or 1.

Note: As an investor, you will want to use the profit line as the baseline. The business owner will want to use the revenue line.

As you are moving through due diligence, you should be noting the overall pros and cons. These are unbelievably valuable when the time comes for determining the valuation.

Another way to look at it is that you are "discounting" the money they have made. Generally, this would not be a business that you make your very first investment in as this type of business would be a salvage operation that has potential but will require work.

An interesting note on valuations is that very rarely do both the business and the investor 100% agree on it.

This is understandable as both sides are motivated by different factors. In addition to emotional attachment and sweat equity, a business owner wants and needs the value of the business to be higher.

This will mean a higher sale price if they are looking to liquidate the business, or a small amount of ownership that they are giving to an investor.

The investor wants the value at the time of investment to be lower because it presents the opportunity to own more for less.

Let's walk through a specific situation. If you as an investor offered to invest $10,000 in exchange for a 10% stake in a business, this by default means that you are valuing the business at $100,000. *$10,000 multiplied by 10 (to make 100%) equals $100,000.*

If you offered the same business $10,000 for a 50% stake, then you are valuing the business at $20,000.

Once the terms have been jointly agreed to, both parties should sign the term sheet.

Chapter Summary/Key Takeaways

In this chapter, we discuss the terms. At this phase, it is all about the details. This is where you are proposing a business marriage. There should be no gaps in the verbal conversations and what is now down on paper. Each of the sections is vital, and they should not be skipped for the sake of making the term sheet shorter. Be brief but don't sell yourself short. Put it all in writing.

CHAPTER TWELVE: PAPERWORK

After the term sheet is signed, there is a brief wait before the deal is finalized.

In this time, use all your powers of observation. Make sure that you are keeping tabs on the businesses, making sure that there are no significant changes to business, including the staff or personnel, the building, the signage, marketing etc.

Look out for large expenditures or purchases. Also, observe the owner's behavior.

Do not feel pressured to sign an agreement sooner than what is allotted for the second level of diligence in the term sheet.

During the waiting period, your attorney should be drafting your agreement.

Be sure to let the attorney know how much time he has to get a draft out. This is especially important if the attorney did not draft the term sheet.

If you are looking to keep the cost of the drafting low, then be sure not to require a rush drafting job and provide all the information that the attorney will need to give you a quality document.

Remember a comprehensive the term sheet is 50% of what makes up a solid agreement.

While I do not recommend that you draft your own agreement, you should know what a comprehensive agreement looks like, and what sections should be included.

The Description of Parties appears at the beginning of the document. This section provides the following information about the buyer(s) and the seller(s):

- Legal names
- Addresses
- Phone numbers

Description Of Business

Also known as the Sellers' Representations and Warranties, this section provides a detailed description of the following things:

- Location(s) of the business
- Purpose of the business
- Services the business provides
- Products the company sells
- Business entity under which the company operates

- Management structure of the business
- Management systems the business uses
- Past, present, and future financials
- Types of customers who come into the business or who use the business's services

Description Of Sale

Absolutely vital to the purchase agreement, this section identifies the following:

- Type of sale (Asset, Stock, Earnout, Seller-Carried Note, and/or Seller Employment)
- Description of every asset, stock, and item included in the sale
- Description of every asset, stock, and item excluded from the sale

Transfer Of Property

Hinging upon the description of sellable assets, stocks, and items, this section can include the following:

- Seller's Agreement to Sell the listed assets, stocks, and items.
- Buyer's Agreement to Purchase the listed assets, stocks, and items.

Purchase Price

Once the document identifies what is, and what is not included in the business sale, the purchase agreement will outline the following:

- Price buyers are paying for the listed assets, items, and/or stocks
- How the buyer plans to pay for the business (can include outside financing, seller-carried notes, seller employment, and/or stock buyouts)

Assumption Of Risk And Liabilities (Sometimes One-And-The-Same As Covenants)

This section often dictates which party assumes responsibility for the following risks and liabilities before and after closing:

- Product loss
- Loss of revenue
- Tax liabilities
- Third-party fees
- Loan obligations
- Vendor obligations
- Employee salaries

Covenants (Often Split Into Buyer Agreements

And Seller Agreements)

If separated from the Assumption of Risk section, many of the protective clauses I mentioned can appear in this section. Look for any:

- **Indemnification**- In business, indemnification is a contractual obligation in which one party agrees to protect another party for financial loss.
- **Business Conduct**- This clause typically states that the business will be run in compliance with all laws.

It may also outline what behaviors will not be tolerated, or what might happen if legal/ criminal action is taken against one of the owners.

- **Non-Compete-** This section will prohibit the owners from starting, participating, or promoting another business in the same sector.

This section may also attempt to restrict the owner from owning a similar business within a specified period.

- **Non-Solicit**- This section will prohibit from selling to or attempting to steal customers, employees, vendors, or other partners from the business.
- **Confidentiality**- This section will protect the data and information of the business from being shared.
- **Intellectual Property**- Generally, the business will own any patents, trademarks, and/or copyrights, even if the individual owner came up with the idea.

A critical section in this agreement details what the seller/ existing business owners' responsibilities are after the agreement is signed.

- Clarify the seller's role within the business after the sale
- Determine who will teach and train the new owners and any new employees
- Specify who will notify vendors and customers that the business has transferred ownership

Participation Or Absence Of Brokers

If buyers and/or sellers have engaged a third-party facilitator or professional during the sale process, the business purchase agreement will detail who those professionals are, and who is responsible for covering their fees. This does include attorney fees.

Conditions

The conditions section will directly mirror the term sheet as all of the conditions should be the same, including what needs to happen for sale to be complete and any due diligence.

Exit

This is important to detail carefully. There should be clarity on how you will exit as an investor even if you plan to be a part of the business indefinitely.

Closing

This section details the when and where the agreement will be executed. It will provide: a location for the closing, list the time closing will occur, issues title transfers (if applicable), and specify what monies will be paid upon closing.

Miscellaneous

The name of the section is a bit misleading. This section is neither unimportant nor unnecessary. This section can include:

Purchase price allocations.

Adjust the purchase price to reflect prorated business expenses, inventory, or accounts receivable on closing day.

Outline how to resolve party disputes if they occur.

Signatures

Appearing at the end of the document, the buyers and sellers will sign their agreement to the terms and conditions outlined in the document.

A representative attorney, banker, broker, or CEPA in attendance at the closing will also sign as a witness and notarize the buyer and seller signatures.

Exhibits/Appendices

This section will include other agreements that would have been requested during the initial diligence period. Any of these documents may be included in this section:

- Financial statements and reports
- The Letter of Intent
- Signed agreements
- Leasehold agreements/transfers
- Vendor agreements/transfers
- Asset valuations
- Owner and/or employee biographies
- Industry reports
- Marketing plans and contracts

It is a good idea that you keep all these documents together, so putting them into the agreement can save you some organizational headaches down the line.

Once the first draft is shared with the business owner, be sure to allow them and their attorney to read, review and make edits.

Do not get frustrated if there are a few rounds of edits. It is far better to have everyone in agreement and on the same page than to encounter a costly conflict down the road.

Chapter Summary/Key Takeaways

In this chapter, we discuss what should be included in your full agreement. When doing this, a good attorney is your best friend. They will cover all the bases and eventualities. As the saying goes, they will draft in the sunshine, and prepare for the rain.

CHAPTER THIRTEEN: THE EXIT

The exit (hopefully) is the fun part of the process. This is the part where your bet and early investment should pay off. If you have followed the procedure carefully, the exit will not be a surprise to either party.
In a typical main street investment, you should be simply cashing out of the business and ownership will likely be back to the original owner.

In a smooth process, the current value of the business will be determined, and your share will be calculated and then paid.

Unfortunately, in the real world, other things can happen.

Here are a few scenarios that you may find yourself in.

Death

If the owner of the business dies, the operating agreement will spell out who will assume the business, or if it will continue.

If the new owner wishes to exit, or has no desire to continue the business, you can cash out before they sell.

This could save you the headache of dealing with a new owner.

Alternatively, if you have had a good experience with the business, you may want to take it over. They may require upfront cash but depending on the new owner, you may be able to structure a buy-out of their interest over time.

Bankruptcy Or Business Closure-

Stuff happens. Whether the cause is an economic recession, a declining neighborhood, or bad business management, the result is the same. In this scenario, you are much more likely to take a financial loss. If the closure is voluntary, meaning not due to a bank foreclosure or another creditor forcing closure, you may be in a position to sell assets and retain some cash.

If the closure is forced, you as an owner will likely have a second- or third-line position for being made whole.

Acquisition

A successful business may attract potential buyers. The majority owner may receive an offer that they could not turn down. If in your agreement, the owner cannot sell without your approval or notifying you—you will have a say in the sale.

If you have no rights to refuse the sale or a first right of refusal (the option to buy the business first), you may want to sell your shares prior to acquisition as there will likely be changes to the business.

Personal Reasons

As an investor, life can happen. Certain personal issues may call for you to sell your interest. The reasons can be a personal financial strain, and you need to find some cash.

A new baby, husband, or relocation can also mean that your investment appetite or risk tolerance has changed.

If this is the case, then you may not be able to capture the full value of what your shares are worth.

Remember that you should always prepare for the exit at the beginning.

When drafting your full agreement, including these scenarios of an untimely exit can save you a lot of time, negotiation, and conflict.

Chapter Summary/Key Takeaways

In this chapter, we talked about the exit. This is the whole point of being an investor. You are making a financial investment and accepting the risks to make a return. If you are acting as an investor, you will not be looking to be a part of the business forever.You are not looking to run a business; you are looking for financial gain.

EPILOGUE/ CONCLUSION

This book is intended to be a guide for first-time investors to get involved in the investment process. Often, communities of color are underinvested in until another group decides to see the value. There are many members of the community that can fill the capital void and help to build value where they live. I hope after reading this book, the process has been demystified, and you realize that we do not need anyone to come and save us—there are angels already among us.

Black Angels in Action

Since the release of Black Angels Among Us 20 new Black Angels have emerged. They have been putting the words into action and are making a difference in their community.

Hilton Williams

Hilton Williams has become active in the community by purchasing land and striking out and becoming an entrepreneur. He has even inspired his son to consider creating a business while in college.

Krystal Peoples "I believe every generation has the obligation to move the next closer to the goal faster and wiser. Every generation I feel a family should grow, get wiser financially, and should set the stage to help the next generation get ahead. My parents worked hard, twelve hour shifts and overtime to make sure I had a brighter future and more options to be successful. My husband had a similar upbringing as well. Therefore it is very important to us to pave the way for the next generation; where it be our own children directly or just future leaders we have the opportunity to connect with and influence. My husband is a natural entrepreneur and has been a business owner now for 3 years proving DJ and entertainment services.

I work in Corporate America and while I do want to climb the corporate ladder; I also want to use my business savviness for other endeavors outside of that to show my own entrepreneurial gifts and together increase income streams for our family. We are committed to leaving a legacy to past on of wealth and knowledge to educate and support future generations to produce income, stand on their own, and identify diverse ways of creating and obtaining wealth."

APPENDIX

Glossary of Common Terms

Sample Due Diligence Questions

Sample Documents

GLOSSARY OF TERMS

1. **Accounts Payable**

Accounts payable is a business finance 101 term. This represents your small business's obligations to pay debts owed to lenders, suppliers, and creditors.

Sometimes referred to as A/P or AP for short, accounts payable can be short or long-term depending upon the type of credit provided to the business by the lender.

2. **Accounts Receivable**

Also known as A/R (or AR, good guess), accounts receivables are another business finance 101 term. It refers to the money owed to your small business by others for goods or services rendered.

These accounts are labeled as assets because they represent a legal obligation for the customer to pay you cash for their short-term debt.

3. **Accrual Basis**

The accrual basis of accounting is an accounting method of recording income when it's actually earned, and expenses when they actually occur.

Accrual basis of accounting is the most common approach used by larger businesses to record and maintain financial transactions.

4. **Accruals**

A business finance term and definition referring to expenses that have been incurred but haven't yet been recorded in the business books. Wages and payroll taxes are common examples.

5. **Asset**

This business finance key term is anything that has value—whether tangible or intangible—and is owned by the business is considered an asset.

Typical items listed as business assets are cash on hand, accounts receivable, buildings, equipment, inventory, and anything else that can be turned into cash.

6. **Balance Sheet**

Along with three other reports relating to the financial health of your small business, the balance sheet is essential information that gives a "snapshot" of the company's net worth at any given time.

The report is a summary of the business assets and liabilities.

7. **Bookkeeping**

A method of accounting that involves the timely recording of all financial transactions for the business.

8. **Capital**

This refers to the overall wealth of a business, as demonstrated by its cash accounts, assets, and investments.

Often called "fixed capital," it refers to the long-term worth of the business.

Capital can be tangible, like durable goods, buildings, and equipment, or intangible such as intellectual property.

9. **Working Capital**

Not to be confused with fixed capital, working capital is another business finance 101 term.

It consists of the financial resources necessary for maintaining the day-to-day operation of the business. Working capital, by definition, is the business's cash on hand, or instruments that you can convert to cash quickly.

10. Cash Flow

Every business needs cash to operate. The business finance term and definition 'cash flow' refers to the amount of operating cash that "flows" through the business and affects the business's liquidity.

Cash flow reports reflect activity for a specified period, usually one accounting period or one month.

Maintaining tight control of cash flow is especially important if your small business is new since ready cash can be limited until the business begins to grow and produce more working capital.

11. **Cash Flow Projections**

Future business decisions will depend on your educated cash flow projections.

To plan for upcoming expenditures and working capital, you need to depend on previous cash flow patterns.

These patterns will give you a comprehensive look at how, and when you receive and spend your cash.

This information is the key to unlock informed, accurate cash flow projections.

12. Depreciation

The value of any asset can be said to depreciate when it loses some of that value in increments over time.

Depreciation occurs due to wear and tear.

Various methods of depreciation are used by businesses to decrease the recorded value of assets.

13. Fixed Asset

A tangible, long-term asset used for the business, and not expected to be sold or otherwise converted into cash during the current or upcoming fiscal year is called a fixed asset.

Fixed assets are items like furniture, computer equipment, equipment, and real estate.

14. Gross Profit

This business finance term and definition can be calculated as total sales (income), less the costs (expenses) directly related to those sales.

Raw materials, manufacturing expenses, labor costs, marketing, and transportation of goods are all included in expenses.

15. Income Statement

Here is one of the four most essential reports lenders and investors want to see when evaluating the viability of your small business.

It is also called a profit and loss statement, and it addresses the business's bottom line, reporting how much the business has earned and spent over a given period.

The result will be either a net gain or a net loss.

16. Intangible Asset

A business asset that is non-physical is considered intangible.

These assets can be items like patents, goodwill, and intellectual property.

17. Liability

This business finance key term is a legal obligation to repay or otherwise settle a debt. Liabilities are considered either current (payable within one year or less) or long-term (payable after one year) and are listed on a business's balance sheet.

A business's accounts payable, wages, taxes, and accrued expenses are all considered liabilities.

18. Liquidity

Liquidity is an indicator of how quickly an asset can be turned into cash for full market value. The more liquid your assets, the more financial flexibility you have.

19. Profit & Loss Statement

See "Income Statement" above.

20. Statement of Cash Flow

One of the essential documents required by lenders and investors that shows a summary of the actual collection of revenue, and payment of expenses for your business.

The statement of cash flow should reflect activity in the areas of operating, investing, and financing, and should be an integral part of your financial statement package.

21. Statement of Shareholders' Equity

If you have chosen to fund your small business with equity financing, and you have established shares and shareholders as part of the controlling interests, you are obligated to provide a financial report that shows changes in the equity section of your balance sheet.

22. Annual Percentage Rate

The business finance term and definition APR represents the real yearly cost of a loan, including all interest and fees.

The total amount of interest to be paid is based on the original amount loaned, or the principal, and is represented in percentage form.

When shopping for the right loan for your small business, you should know the APR for the loan in question. This figure can be helpful in comparing one financial tool with another since it represents the actual cost of borrowing.

23. Appraisal

Just like your real estate appraisal when buying a house, an appraisal is a professional opinion of market value.

When closing a loan for your small business, you will probably need one or more of the three types of appraisals: real estate, equipment, and business value.

24. Balloon Loan

A loan that is structured in a way that the small business owner makes regular repayments on a predetermined schedule, and one much larger payment or balloon payment, at the end.

These can be attractive to new businesses because the payments are smaller at the outset when the business is more likely to be facing strict financial constraints.

However, be sure that your business will be capable of making that last balloon payment since it will be a large one.

25. Bankruptcy

This federal law is used as a tool for businesses or individuals who are having severe financial challenges.

It provides a plan for reduction and repayment of debts over time, or an opportunity to eliminate the majority of the outstanding debts completely.

Turning to bankruptcy should be given careful thought because it will hurt the business credit score.

26. Bootstrapping

Using your own money to finance the start-up and growth of your small business. Think of it as being your own investor.

Once the business is up and running successfully, the business finance term and definition bootstrapping refers to the use of profits earned to reinvest in the business.

27. Business Credit Report

Just like you have a personal credit report that lenders look at to determine risk factors for making personal loans, businesses also generate credit reports.

These are maintained by credit bureaus that record information about a business's financial history.

Items like how large the company is, how long it has been in business, amount and type of credit issued to the business, how credit has been managed, and any legal filings (i.e., bankruptcy) are all questions addressed by the business credit report.

Lenders, investors, and insurance companies use these reports to evaluate risk exposure and financial health of a business.

28. Business Credit Score

A business credit score is calculated based on the information found in the business credit report.

Using a specialized algorithm, business credit scoring companies take into account all the information found on your credit report and give your small business a credit score.

Also called a commercial credit score, this number is used by various lenders and suppliers to evaluate your creditworthiness.

29. Collateral

Any asset that you pledge as security for a loan instrument is called collateral.

Lenders often require collateral as a way to make sure they won't lose money if your business defaults on the loan.

When you pledge an asset for collateral, it becomes subject to seizure by the lender if you fail to meet the requirements of the loan documents.

30. Credit Limit

When a lender offers a business line of credit, it usually comes with a credit limit, or a maximum amount that you can use at any given time.

It is said that you reach your credit limit or "max out" your credit when you borrow up to or exceed that number.

A business line of credit can be especially useful if your business is seasonal, or if the income is extremely unpredictable.

It is one of the fastest ways to access cash for emergencies.

31. Debt Consolidation

If your small business has several loans with various payments, you might want to consider a business debt consolidation loan.

It is a process that lets you combine multiple loans into a single loan.

The advantages are possibly reducing the interest rates on the borrowed funds, as well as lowering the total amount you repay each month.

Businesses use this tool to help improve cash flow.

32. Debt Service Coverage Ratio

The business finance term and definition debt service coverage ratio (DSCR) are the ratio of cash your small business has available for paying or servicing its debt.

Debt payments include making principal and interest payments on the loan you are requesting.

Generally speaking, if your DSCR is above 1, your business has enough income to meet its debt requirements.

33. Debt Financing

When you borrow money from a lender and agree to repay the principal with interest in regular payments for a specified period, you're using debt financing.

Traditionally, it has been the most common form of funding for small businesses.

Debt financing can include borrowing from banks, business credit cards, lines of credit, personal loans, merchant cash advances, and invoice financing.

This method creates a debt that must be repaid, but lets you maintain sole control of your business.

34. Equity Financing

The act of using investor funds in exchange for a piece or" share" of your business is another way to raise capital.

These funds can come from friends, family, angel investors, or venture capitalists.

Before deciding to use equity financing to raise the cash necessary for your business, determine how much control you are willing to share when it comes to decision-making and philosophy.

Some investors will also want voting rights.

35. FICO Score

A FICO score is another type of credit score used by potential lenders for evaluating the wisdom of entering a contract with you and your business. The Fair Isaac Corporation created it, hence the name FICO.

FICO scores comprise a substantial part of the credit report that lenders use to assess credit risk.

36. Financial Statements

An integral part of the loan application process is furnishing information that shows your business is a good credit risk.

The standard financial statement packet includes four main reports: the income statement, the balance sheet, the statement of cash flow, and the statement of shareholders' equity, if you have shareholders.

Lenders and investors want to see that your business is well-balanced with assets and liabilities, has positive cash flow, and will have the capital to make expected repayments.

37. Fixed Interest Rate

The interest rate on a loan that is established in the beginning and does not change for the lifetime of the loan is said to be fixed.

Loans with fixed interest rates are appealing to small business owners because the repayment amounts are consistent and easier to budget for in the future.

38. Floating Interest Rate

In contrast to the business finance term and definition fixed rate, the floating interest rate will change with market fluctuations.

Also referred to as variable rates or adjustable rates, these amounts may often start out lower than the fixed-rate percentages. This makes them more appealing in the short term if the market is trending down.

39. Guarantor

When starting a new small business, lenders might want you to provide a guarantor. This is an individual who guarantees to cover the balance owed on a debt if you or your business cannot meet the repayment obligation.

40. Interest Rate

All loans and other lending instruments are assigned the business finance key term interest rates. This is a percentage of the principal amount charged by the lender for the use of its money.

Interest rates represent the current cost of borrowing.

41. Invoice Factoring or Financing

If your business has a significant number of open invoices outstanding, you may contact a factoring company and have them purchase the invoices at a discount.

By raising capital this way, there is no debt, and the factoring company assumes the financial responsibility for collecting the invoice debts.

42. Lien

This business finance term and definition is a creditor's legal claim to the collateral pledged as security for a loan is called a lien.

43. Line of Credit

A lender may offer you an unsecured amount of funds available for your business to draw on when capital is needed.

This line of credit is considered a short-term funding option, with a maximum amount available.

This pre-approved pool of money is appealing because it gives you quick access to the cash.

44. Loan-to-Value

The LTV comparison is a ratio of the fair market value of an asset compared to the amount of the loan that will fund it.

This is another critical number for lenders who need to know if the value of the asset will cover the loan repayment if your business defaults and fails to pay.

45. Long-Term Debt

Any loan product with a total repayment schedule lasting longer than one year is considered long-term debt.

46. Merchant Cash Advance

A merchant may offer a funding method through a loan based on the business's monthly sales volume. Repayment is made with a percentage of the daily or weekly sales.

These tend to be short-term loans and are one of the costliest ways to fund your small business.

47. Microloan

Microloans are loans made through nonprofit, community-based organizations, and they are most often for amounts under $50,000.

48. Personal Guarantee

If you're seeking financing for a very new business, and don't have a high-value asset to offer as collateral, you may be asked by the lender to sign a statement of personal guarantee.

In effect, this statement affirms that you, as an individual, will act as guarantor for the business's debt, making you personally liable for the balance of the loan, even if the business fails.

49. Principal

Any loan instrument is made of three parts—the principal, the interest, and the fees.

The principal is a business finance key term and is the original amount that is borrowed or the outstanding balance to be re-paid less interest.

It is used to calculate the total interest and fees charged.

50. Revolving Line of Credit

This business finance term and definition is a funding option and is similar to a standard line of credit.

However, the agreement is to lend a specific amount of money, and once that sum is repaid, it can be borrowed again.

51. Secured Loan

Many lenders will require some form of security when loaning money. When this happens, this business finance term and definition is a secured loan.

The asset being used as collateral for the loan is said to be "securing" the loan.

If your small business defaults on the loan, the lender can then claim the collateral, and use its fair-market value to offset the unpaid balance.

52. Term Loan

These are debt financing tools used to raise needed funds for your small business.

Term loans provide the business with a lump sum of cash upfront in exchange for a promise to repay the principal and interest at specified intervals over a set period.

These are typically longer-term, one-time loans for start-up expenses or costs for established business expansion.

53. Unsecured Loans

Loans that are not backed by collateral are called unsecured loans.

These types of loans represent a higher risk for the lender, so you can expect to pay higher interest rates and have shorter repayment time frames.

Credit cards are an excellent example of unsecured loans that are a good option for small business funding when combined with other financing options.

54. Articles of Incorporation

This is legal documentation of the business's creation, including name, type of business, and type of business structure or incorporation.

This paperwork is one of the first tasks you will complete when you officially start your business.

Once submitted, your articles of incorporation are kept on file with the appropriate governmental agencies.

55. Business Plan

Here is your tool for demonstrating how you want to establish your small business, and how you plan to grow it into good financial health.

When writing a business plan, it should include financial, operational, and marketing goals as well as how you plan to get there.

The more specific you are with your business plan, the better prepared you will be in the long run.

56. Employer Identification Number (EIN) Certificate

In order to be more easily identified by the Internal Revenue Service, every business entity is assigned a unique number called an EIN.

When you start your small business, an EIN will be assigned and mailed to the business address.

This number never changes, and you will be asked to furnish it for many reasons.

57. Franchise Agreement

For a small business entrepreneur, entering into a franchise agreement with a larger company can be a way to enter the marketplace.

The agreement made between you and the larger company gives you the right to operate as a satellite of the larger company in a defined territory for a given period.

This lets you, the business owner, take advantage of a brand name that's already familiar in the marketplace, and a process or operation that has already been tested.

58. Net Worth

This business finance term and definition is an expression of your business's total value, as determined by your total current assets less the total liabilities currently owned by the business.

With your business's most recent balance sheet in hand, you can calculate the net worth using a simple formula: Assets – Liabilities = Net Worth.

59. Retained Earnings

Just like it sounds, this term represents any profits earned that are retained in the business.

This can also be referred to as bootstrapping.

60. Tax Lien

If your business fails to pay taxes owed to the designated government entity, namely the IRS, you may find your assets seized by the claim of a tax lien.

The government can not only seize your assets for liquidation to resolve the tax debt, but they can also charge you penalties on the amount you owe.

SAMPLE DUE DILIGENCE QUESTIONS

Sample Due Diligence Request Checklist

Set forth below, is a preliminary list of documents and information regarding [Company Name] (together with all subsidiaries and any predecessors, collectively, the "Company") which must be reviewed by Buyer, Inc. ("Buyer") and its counsel and advisors in connection with a possible transaction with the Company. This is not a definitive list, and as the review proceeds, additional items may be requested.

Please assemble and deliver the documents and information requested below for our review as soon as possible.

Unless otherwise indicated, documents should be made available for all periods subsequent to [XX] years and should include all amendments, supplements and other ancillary documents.

Please provide all other requested information or documents. If any of the items requested does not exist or is not relevant to the Company, please note this be placing the words "NONE" or "NOT APPLICABLE" below the listed item.

A. ORGANIZATION OF THE COMPANY

1. Describe the corporate or other structure of the legal entities that comprise the Company. Include any helpful diagrams or

charts. Provide a list of the officers and directors of the Company and a brief description of their duties.

2. Long-form certificate of good standing and articles or certificate of incorporation from Secretary of State or other appropriate official in the Company's jurisdiction of incorporation, listing all documents on file with respect to the Company, and a copy of all documents listed therein.

3. Current by-laws of the Company.

4. List of all jurisdictions in which the Company is qualified to do business and list of all other jurisdictions in which the Company owns or leases real property or maintains an office and a description of business in each such jurisdiction. Copies of the certificate of authority, good standing certificates and tax status certificates from all jurisdictions in which the Company is qualified to do business.

5. All minutes for meetings of the Company's board of directors, board committees and stockholders for the last [five] years, and all written actions or consents in lieu of meetings thereof.

6. List of all subsidiaries and other entities (including partnerships) in which the Company has an equity interest; organizational chart showing ownership of such entities; and any agreements relating to the Company's interest in any such entity.

B. OWNERSHIP AND CONTROL OF THE COMPANY

1. Capitalization of the Company, including all outstanding capital stock, convertible securities, options, warrants and similar instruments.

2. List of security holders of the Company (including option and warrant holders), setting forth class and number of securities held.

3. Copies of any voting agreements, stockholder agreements, proxies, transfer restriction agreements, rights of first offer or refusal, preemptive rights, registration agreements or other

agreements regarding the ownership or control of the Company.

C. ASSETS AND OPERATIONS

1. Annual financial statements with notes thereto for the past three fiscal years of the Company, and the latest interim financial statements since the end of the last fiscal year and product sales and cost of sales (including royalties) analysis for each product which is part of assets to be sold.

2. All current budgets and projections including projections for product sales and cost of sales.

3. Any auditors (internal and external) letters and reports to management for the past [five] years (and management's responses thereto).

4. Provide a detailed breakdown of the basis for the allowance for doubtful accounts.

5. Inventory valuation, including turnover rates and statistics, gross profit percentages and obsolescence analyses including inventory of each product which is part of assets to be sold.

6. Letters to auditors from outside counsel.

7. Description of any real estate owned by the Company and copies of related deeds, surveys, title insurance policies (and all documents referred to therein), title opinions, certificates of occupancy, easements, zoning variances, condemnation or eminent domain orders or proceedings, deeds of trust, mortgages and fixture lien filings.

8. Schedule of significant fixed assets, owned or used by the Company, including the identification of the person holding title to such assets and any material liens or restrictions on such assets.

9. Without duplication from Section D below, or separate intellectual property due diligence checklist, schedule of all intangible assets (including customer lists and goodwill) and proprietary or intellectual properties owned or used in the Company,

including a statement as to the entity holding title or right to such assets and any material liens or restrictions on such assets. Include on and off-balance sheet items.

D. INTELLECTUAL PROPERTY

List of all patents, trademarks, trade names, service marks and copyrights owned or used by the

Company, all applications there for and copies thereof, search reports related thereto and information about any liens or other restrictions and agreements on or related to any of the foregoing (without duplication from attached intellectual property due diligence checklist).

E. REPORTS

1. Copies of any studies, appraisals, reports, analyses or memoranda within the last [three]years relating to the Company (i.e., competition, products, pricing, technological developments, software developments, etc.).

2. Current descriptions of the Company that may have been prepared for any purpose, including any brochures used in soliciting or advertising.

3. Descriptions of any customer quality awards, plant qualification/certification distinctions, ISO certifications or other awards or certificates viewed by the Company as significant or reflective of superior performance.

4. Copies of any analyst or other market reports concerning the Company known to have been issued within the last [three] years.

5. Copies of any studies prepared by the Company regarding the Company's insurance currently in effect and self-insurance program (if any), together with information on the claim and loss experience there under.

6. Any of the following documents filed by the Company or affiliates of the Company and which contain information con-

cerning the Company: annual reports on SEC Form 10-K; quarterly reports on SEC Form 10-Q; current reports on SEC Form 8-K.

F. COMPLIANCE WITH LAWS

1. Copies of all licenses, permits, certificates, authorizations, registrations, concessions, approvals, exemptions and other operating authorities from all governmental authorities and any applications there for, and a description of any pending contemplated or threatened changes in the foregoing.

2. A description of any pending or threatened proceedings or investigations before any court or any regulatory authority.

3. Describe any circumstance where the Company has been or may be accused of violating any law or failing to possess any material license, permit or other authorization.

List all citations and notices from governmental or regulatory authorities.

4. Schedule of the latest dates of inspection of the Company's facilities by each regulatory authority that has inspected such facilities.

5. Description of the potential effect on the Company of any pending or proposed regulatory changes of which the Company is aware.

6. Copies of any information requests from, correspondence with, reports of or to, filings with or other material information with respect to any regulatory bodies which regulate a material portion of the Company's business. Limit response to the last [five] years unless an older document has a continuing impact on the Company.

7. Copies of all other studies, surveys, memoranda or other data on regulatory compliance including: spill control, environmental clean-up or environmental preventive or remedial matters, employee safety compliance, import or export licenses, com-

mon carrier licenses, problems, potential violations, expenditures, etc.

8. State whether any consent is necessary from any governmental authority to embark upon or consummate the proposed transaction.

9. Schedule of any significant U.S. import or export restrictions that relate to the Company's operations.

10. List of any export, import or customs permits or authorizations, certificates, registrations, concessions, exemptions, etc., that are required in order for the Company to conduct its business and copies of all approvals, etc. granted to the Company that are currently in effect or pending renewal.

11. Any correspondence with or complaints from third parties relating to the marketing, sales or promotion practices of the Company.

G. ENVIRONMENTAL MATTERS

1. A list of facilities or other properties currently or formerly owned, leased, or operated by the Company and its predecessors, if any.

2. Reports of environmental audits or site assessments in the possession of the Company, including any Phase I or Phase II assessments or asbestos surveys, relating to any such facilities or properties.

3. Copies of any inspection reports prepared by any governmental agency or insurance carrier in connection with environmental or workplace safety and health regulations relating to any such facilities or properties.

4. Copies of all environmental and workplace safety and health notices of violations, complaints, consent decrees, and other documents indicating noncompliance with environmental or workplace safety and health laws or regulations, received by the Company from local, state, or federal governmental author-

ities. If available, include documentation indicating how such situations were resolved.

5. Copies of any private party complaints, claims, lawsuits or other documents relating to potential environmental liability of the Company to private parties.

6. Listing of underground storage tanks currently or previously present at the properties and facilities listed in response to Item 1 above, copies of permits, licenses or registrations relating to such tanks, and documentation of underground storage tank removals and any associated remediation work.

7. Descriptions of any release of hazardous substances or petroleum known by the Company to have occurred at the properties and facilities listed in response to Item 1, if such release has not otherwise been described in the documents provided in response to Items 1-6 above.

8. Copies of any information requests, PRP notices, "106 orders," or other notices received by the Company pursuant to CERCLA or similar state or foreign laws relating to liability for hazardous substance releases at off-site facilities.

9. Copies of any notices or requests described in Item 8 above, relating to potential liability for hazardous substance releases at any properties or facilities described in response to Item 1.

10. Copies of material correspondence or other documents (including any relating to the Company's share of liability) with respect to any matters identified in response to Items 8 and 9.

11. Copies of any written analyses conducted by the Company or an outside consultant relating to future environmental activities (i.e., upgrades to control equipment, improvements in waste disposal practices, materials substitution) for which expenditure of funds greater than [$XX,000] is either certain or reasonably anticipated within the next [five] years and an estimate of the costs associated with such activities.

12. Description of the workplace safety and health programs currently in place for the Company's business, with particular emphasis on chemical handling practices.

H. LITIGATION

1. List of all litigation, arbitration and governmental proceedings relating to the Company to which the Company or any of its directors, officers or employees is or has been a party, or which is threatened against any of them, indicating the name of the court, agency or other body before whom pending, date instituted, amount involved, insurance coverage and current status. Also describe any similar matters which were material to the Company, and which were adjudicated or settled in the last [ten] years.

2. Information as to any past or present governmental investigation of or proceeding involving the Company or the Company's directors, officers or employees.

3. Copies of all attorneys' responses to audit inquiries.

4. Copies of any consent decrees, orders (including applicable injunctions) or similar documents to which the Company is a party, and a brief description of the circumstances surrounding such document.

5. Copies of all letters of counsel to independent public accountants concerning pending or threatened litigation.

6. Any reports or correspondence related to the infringement by the Company or a third party of intellectual property rights.

I. SIGNIFICANT CONTRACTS AND COMMITMENTS

1. Contracts relating to any completed (during the past 10 years) or proposed reorganization, acquisition, merger, or purchase or sale of substantial assets (including all agreements relating to the sale, proposed acquisition or disposition of any and all divisions, subsidiaries or businesses) of or with respect to the Company.

2. All joint venture and partnership agreements to which the Company is a party.

3. All material agreements encumbering real or personal property owned by the Company including mortgages, pledges, security agreements or financing statements.

4. Copies of all real property leases relating to the Company (whether the Company is lessor or lessee), and all leasehold title insurance policies (if any).

5. Copies of all leases of personal property and fixtures relating to the Company (whether the Company is lessor or lessee), including, without limitation, all equipment rental agreements.

6. Guarantees or similar commitments by or on behalf of the Company, other than endorsements for collection in the ordinary course and consistent with past practice.

7. Indemnification contracts or arrangements insuring or indemnifying any director, officer, employee or agent against any liability incurred in such capacity.

8. Loan agreements, notes, industrial revenue bonds, compensating balance arrangements, lines of credit, lease financing arrangements, installment purchases, etc. relating to the Company or its assets and copies of any security interests or other liens securing such obligations.

9. No-default certificates and similar documents delivered to lenders for the last [five] (or shorter period, if applicable) years evidencing compliance with financing agreements.

10. Documentation used internally for the last [five] years (or shorter time period, if applicable) to monitor compliance with financial covenants contained in financing agreements.

11. Any correspondence or documentation for the last [five] years (or shorter period, if applicable) relating to any defaults or potential defaults under financing agreements.

12. Contracts involving cooperation with other companies or

restricting competition.

13. Contracts relating to other material business relationships, including: a. any current service, operation or maintenance contracts; b. any current contracts with customers; c. any current contracts for the purchase of fixed assets; and d; any franchise, distributor or agency contracts.

14. Without duplicating Section d above or the intellectual property due diligence schedule hereto, contracts involving licensing, know-how or technical assistance arrangements including contracts relating to any patent, trademark, service mark and copyright registrations or other proprietary rights used by the Company and any other agreement under which royalties are to be paid or received.

15. Description of any circumstances under which the Company may be required to repurchase or repossess assets or properties previously sold.

16. Data processing agreements relating to the Company.

17. Copies of any contract by which any broker or finder is entitled to a fee for facilitating the proposed transaction or any other transactions involving the Company or its properties or assets.

18. Management, service or support agreements relating to the Company, or any power of attorney with respect to any material assets or aspects of the Company.

19. List of significant vendor and service providers (if any) who, for whatever reason, expressly decline to do business with the Company.

20. Samples of all forms, including purchase orders, invoices, supply agreements, etc.

21. Any agreements or arrangements relating to any other transactions between the Company and any director, officer, stockholder or affiliate of the Company (collectively, "Related Per-

sons"), including but not limited to:

a. Contracts or understandings between the Company and any Related Person regarding the sharing of assets, liabilities, services, employee benefits, insurance, data processing, third-party consulting, professional services or intellectual property.

b. Contracts or understandings between Related Persons and third parties who supply inventory or services through Related Persons to the Company.

c. Contracts or understandings between the Company and any Related Person that contemplate favorable pricing or terms to such parties.

d. Contracts or understandings between the Company and any Related Person regarding the use of hardware or software.

e. Contracts or understandings regarding the maintenance of equipment of any Related Person that is either sold, rented, leased or used by the Company.

f. Description of the percentage of business done by the Company with Related Persons.

g. Covenants not to compete and confidentiality agreements between the Company and a Related Person.

h. List of all accounts receivable, loans and other obligations owing to or by the Company from or to a Related Person, together with any agreements relating there to.

22. Copies of all insurance and indemnity policies and coverages carried by the Company including policies or coverages for products, properties, business risk, casualty and workers compensation. A description of any self-insurance or retro-premium plan or policy, together with the costs thereof for the last [five] years. A summary of all material claims for the last [five] years as well as aggregate claims experience data and studies.

23. List of any other agreements or group of related agreements

with the same party or group of affiliated parties continuing over a period of more than six months from the date or dates thereof, not terminable by the Company on 30 days' notice.

24. Copies of all supply agreements relating to the Company and a description of any supply arrangements.

25. Copies of all contracts relating to marketing and advertising.

26. Copies of all construction agreements and performance guarantees.

27. Copies of all secrecy, confidentiality and nondisclosure agreements.

28. Copies of all agreements related to the development or acquisition of technology.

29. Copies of all agreements outside the ordinary course of business.

30. Copies of all warranties offered by the Company with respect to its product or services.

31. List of all major contracts or understandings not otherwise previously disclosed under this section, indicating the material terms and parties.

32. For any contract listed in this Section I, state whether any party is in default or claimed to be in default.

33. For any contract listed in this Section I, state whether the contract requires the consent of any person to assign such contract or collaterally assign such contract to any lender.

NOTE: Remember to include all amendments, schedules, exhibits and side letters. Also include brief description of any oral contract listed in this Section I.

J. EMPLOYEES, BENEFITS AND CONTRACTS

1. Copies of the Company's employee benefit plans as most

recently amended, including all pension, profit sharing, thrift, stock bonus, ESOPs, health and welfare plans (including retiree health), bonus, stock option plans, direct or deferred compensation plans and severance plans, together with the following documents:

a. all applicable trust agreements for the foregoing plans.

b. copies of all IRS determination letter for the foregoing qualified plans;

c. latest IRS forms for the foregoing qualified plans, including all annual reports, schedules and attachments.

d. latest copies of all summary plan descriptions, including modifications, for the foregoing plans.

e. latest actuarial evaluations with respect to the foregoing defined benefit plans; and

f. schedule of fund assets and unfunded liabilities under applicable plans.

2. Copies of all employment contracts, consulting agreements, severance agreements, independent contractor agreements, non-disclosure agreements and non-compete agreements relating to any employees of the Company.

3. Copies of any collective bargaining agreements and related plans and trusts relating to the Company (if any). Description of labor disputes relating to the Company within the last [three] years. List of current organizational efforts and projected schedule of future collective bargaining negotiations (if any).

4. Copies of all employee handbooks and policy manuals (including affirmative action plans).

5. Copies of all OSHA examinations, reports or complaints.

6. The results of any formal employee surveys.

K. TAX MATTERS

1. Copies of returns for the three prior closed tax years and all open tax years for the Company (including all federal and state consolidated returns) together with a work paper there for wherein each item is detailed and documented that reconciles net income.

as specified in the applicable financial statement with taxable income for the related period.

2. Audit and revenue agents reports for the Company; audit adjustments proposed by the Internal Revenue Service for any audited tax year of the Company or by any other taxing authority; or protests filed by the Company.

3. Settlement documents and correspondence for last [six] years involving the Company.

4. Agreements waiving statute of limitations or extending time involving the Company.

5. Description of accrued federal, state and local withholding taxes and FICA for the Company.

6. List of all state, local and foreign jurisdictions in which the Company pays taxes or collects sales taxes from its retail customers (specifying which taxes are paid or collected in each jurisdiction).

L. MISCELLANEOUS

1. Information regarding any material contingent liabilities and material unasserted claims and information regarding any asserted or unasserted violation of any employee safety and environmental laws and any asserted or unasserted pollution clean-up liability.

2. List of the ten largest customers and suppliers for each product or service of the Company.

3. List of major competitors for each business segment or product line.

4. Any plan or arrangement filed or confirmed under the federal bankruptcy laws, if any.

5. A list of all officers, directors and stockholders of the Company.

6. All annual and interim reports to stockholders and any other communications with security holders.

7. Description of principal banking and credit relationships (excluding payroll matters), including the names of each bank or other financial institution, the nature, limit and current status of any outstanding indebtedness, loan or credit commitment and other financing arrangements.

8. Summary and description of all product, property, business risk, employee health, group life and key-man insurance.

9. Copies of any UCC or other lien, judgment or suit searches or filings related to the Company in relevant states conducted in the past [three] years.

10. Copies of all filings with the Securities and Exchange Commission, state blue sky authorities or foreign security regulators or exchanges.

11. All other information material to the financial condition, businesses, assets, prospects or commercial relations of the Company.

NON-DISCLOSURE AGREEMENT

XXX, LLC

Nondisclosure Agreement

This Nondisclosure Agreement (the "Agreement") is entered into by and between ______________________________, a ____ ____ [STATE & ENTITY TYPE] ("YOU"), and **XXX, LLC**, a North Carolina Limited Liability Partnership ("XX"), collectively referred to as the "Parties", for the purpose of preventing the unauthorized disclosure of Confidential Information as defined below. The Parties agree to enter into a confidential relationship with respect to the disclosure by one or each (the "Disclosing Party") to the other (the "Receiving Party") of certain proprietary and confidential information ("Confidential Information").

1. **Definition of Confidential Information**. For purposes of this Agreement, "Confidential Information" shall include all information or material that has or could have commercial value or other utility in any business in which either Party is engaged. If Confidential Information is in written form, the Disclosing Party shall label or stamp the materials with the word "Confidential" or some similar warning. If Confidential Information is transmitted orally, the Disclosing Party shall promptly provide a writing indicating that such oral communication constituted Confidential Information.

2. **Exclusions from Confidential Information**. Receiving

Party's obligations under this Agreement do not extend to information that is: (a) publicly known at the time of disclosure or subsequently becomes publicly known through no fault of the Receiving Party; (b) discovered or created by the Receiving Party before disclosure by Disclosing Party; (c) learned by the Receiving Party through legitimate means other than from the Disclosing Party or Disclosing Party's representatives; or (d) is disclosed by Receiving Party with Disclosing Party's prior written approval.

3. **Obligations of Receiving Party**. Receiving Party shall hold and maintain the Confidential Information in strictest confidence for the sole and exclusive benefit of the Disclosing Party. Receiving Party shall carefully restrict access to Confidential Information to employees, contractors, and third parties as is reasonably required and shall require those persons to sign nondisclosure restrictions at least as protective as those in this Agreement. Receiving Party shall not, without prior written approval of Disclosing Party, use for Receiving Party's own benefit, publish, copy, or otherwise disclose to others, or permit the use by others for their benefit or to the detriment of Disclosing Party, any Confidential Information. Receiving Party shall return to Disclosing Party any and all records, notes, and other written, printed, or tangible materials in its possession pertaining to Confidential Information immediately if Disclosing Party requests it in writing.

4. **Time Periods**. The nondisclosure provisions of this Agreement shall survive the termination of this Agreement and Receiving Party's duty to hold Confidential Information in confidence shall remain in effect until the Confidential Information no longer qualifies as a trade secret or until Disclosing Party sends Receiving Party written notice releasing Receiving Party from this Agreement, whichever occurs first.

5. **Relationships**. Nothing contained in this Agreement shall be deemed to constitute either Party a partner, joint-ven-

turer or employee of the other Party for any purpose.

6. **Severability**. If a court finds any provision of this Agreement invalid or unenforceable, the remainder of this Agreement shall be interpreted so as best to effect the intent of the Parties.

7. **Integration**. This Agreement expresses the complete understanding of the Parties with respect to the subject matter and supersedes all prior proposals, agreements, representations, and understandings. This Agreement may not be amended except in a writing signed by both Parties.

8. **Waiver**. The failure to exercise any right provided in this Agreement shall not be a waiver of prior or subsequent rights.

EACH NAMED PARTY EXPRESSLY AGREES THAT THE DISCLOSURE OF THE CONFIDENTIAL INFORMATION BY THE DISCLOSING PARTY IS THE SOLE REASON FOR ITS ENTRY INTO THIS NONDISCLOSURE AGREEMENT.

This Agreement and each Party's obligations shall be binding on the representatives, assigns, and successors of such Party. Each Party has signed this Agreement through its authorized representative.

ACKNOWLEDGED:

____

Signature: ______________________________________

Title: _____________

Name: ______________________________________

Date: _____________

<u>XXX, LLC</u>

Signature: ______________________________________

Title: _____________

Name: ______________________________________

Date: _____________

OPERATING AGREEMENT

Operating Agreement

XXX LLC

This Operating Agreement, referred to herein as the Agreement, is made this 1st day of January 2018 by and between XXX, a resident of Charlotte, North Carolina, and XXXX, a resident of Charlotte, North Carolina, who are referred to herein the Members.

The Members have formed a Limited Liability Company, which is known as Off the Vine Juices and Smoothies, LLC under the laws of the North Carolina, and which is referred to herein as the Company. The two Members listed in the preceding paragraph are the only Members of the Company. In consideration of the mutual promises contained in this Agreement, and in order to establish procedures for operating the Company and intending to be legally bound by the terms and conditions set forth herein, the Members hereby agree as follows.

A. The Company and its Business

1. The primary business to be conducted by the Company shall be the selling of healthy beverage made from fruits and vegetables. The Company may also engage in any other lawful business that the Members may approve.
2. The name of the Company shall be registered with the Office of the Secretary of State of the [State]

3. The registered office of the Company, and its principal place of business shall be located at [address], which is the location of the first store.
4. Each member shall devote time to the business. The business will maintain regular working hours, each Member will work whatever hours that are required to accomplish their respective responsibilities as set forth in this Agreement.

B. Capital Contributions

5. Each Member shall make equal contributions to the capital of the Company. Subsequent capital contributions shall be provided by each Member as may be required from time to time to operate the Company's business adequately.
6. Each Member shall own an equal 50% share of the Company and its business.

C. Accountability

7. The responsibilities for each Member's role in operating the Company's business are set forth in more detail later in this Agreement. Charmaine is responsible for store operations and coordination. Christopher is responsible for providing ancillary support for the business. Each Member shall be accountable to the other Member for the satisfactory performance of their responsibilities and shall devote whatever time and effort that may be required to accomplish the goals that may be established by mutual agreement between the Members from time to time.
8. The Company is organized as a Limited Liability Company (LLC) pursuant to the Business Corporation Law of [State]. Having two Members, the Company shall be taxed by the Internal Revenue Service as a Membership.

D. Liability

9. The personal liability of each Member shall be limited

to their respective investment in the Company. The Members shall not be subject to joint and several liability as would affect the general Members in a general Membership.

10. The Company subscribes to the highest personal standards of ethical conduct in any activity related to the Company's business. Any improper, unethical or illegal activity undertaken by either Member shall be deemed to have been disavowed by the Company and shall not affect the liability of the other Member. One Member shall not be held liable for the illegal activity of the other Member, provided the innocent Member had no knowledge or participation in such illegal activity.
11. Each Member shall be personally responsible for 50% of any debt that is incurred legitimately by the Company.

E. Authority

12. a. The Members shall meet at least once a week, at a time that is mutually agreeable, at the office of the Company, to discuss the business of the Company. Each Member shall have an equal vote in making decisions affecting the conduct of the Company's business. All decisions shall be made by consensus. In order to avoid a possible impasse or deadlock, in the event that the Members are unable to agree on a major business decision, the matter shall be submitted for decision by the accountant who is retained by the Company to keep its books. The decision of the accountant shall be binding upon the Members. If, for any reason, the accountant is unable or unwilling to make such a decision, the matter in controversy shall be referred to the lawyer who represents the Company, whose decision

shall be binding upon the Members.

b. Each Member is authorized to make decisions affecting his/her area of responsibility, as set forth in Section F, below, in the normal course of business, without consulting the other Member, provided the decision does not exceed the amount of $5,000.00. Any decision affecting more than $5,000.00 must have the prior approval of the other Member.

c. The Company shall be managed directly by its Members.

15. Either Member may sign a check drawn on the Company's bank account, provided the amount of the transaction does not exceed $5,000.00. Both Members must sign any check in an amount more than $5,000.00.

F. Responsibilities

14. Individual workloads will be established at the weekly meetings of the Members as set forth in Section 12 a., above. Each Member is encouraged to exercise individual initiative in order to achieve the goals of the Company and provide for its prosperity.

G. Personnel

15. The selection of professional service providers, such as accountant, lawyer, insurance agent and banker, shall be made by consensus between the Members.

16. New Members shall be admitted to the Company only by unanimous agreement among the existing Members. As a condition of membership in the Company, new Members shall be required to execute a Joinder Agreement, whereby they subscribe to all the terms and conditions of this Operating Agreement, or whatever version hereof is in effect at the time.

17. Employees and/or independent contractors shall be hired by the Members as the needs of the business may require.

18. Vendors and/or suppliers of goods or services that may

be required by the Company may be selected by either Member as needed.

19. Buyers of the Company's merchandise may be selected by either Member.

H. Insurance

20. General liability insurance will be secured in line with state laws.

21. Employee benefits, such as life insurance, disability insurance, pensions and any other similar benefits shall be provided as the Members may decide by mutual agreement.

I. Ownership and Compensation

22. Each Member owns an equal 50% interest in the Company and its business. In the event that new Members are admitted, pursuant to the provisions of Section 17, above, new Membership interests shall be determined and allocated by the unanimous agreement of all existing Members.
23. Compensation and distribution of profits shall be made to the Members in equal shares, unless otherwise agreed by mutual consent.
24. Any losses incurred by the Company shall be allocated among the Members in equal shares, unless otherwise agreed my mutual consent.
25. The retention of profits for reinvestment in the Company's business from time to time shall be made as the Members may agree unanimously.
26. Salaries for the Members and any employees that may be hired shall be established and paid as the Members may determine by unanimous agreement.
27. Company perquisites, such as company-owned cars and similar benefits, shall be provided to Members and/or employees as the Members may determine by unanimous decision.

28. Employee benefits such as vacation, paid holidays, sick time, family time, mental health time and similar benefits shall be provided, as the Members shall determine by unanimous decision.
29. Conditions which affect a Member's ability to work productively, such as serious illness, disability or other unexpected situation shall be dealt with as the Members may decide by mutual agreement.
30. Any extended absence from work of a Member, which adversely affects the performance of the Company and/or its business, shall be dealt with as the need arises in such manner as the Members may decide by mutual agreement. The continuation of pay and benefits during any such period of extended absence from work or disability shall be subject to unanimous agreement among all Members.
31. Pursuant to the provisions above, the books of account shall be kept by Charmaine. An accountant shall be selected by the Members to prepare regular financial reports and tax returns for the Company.
32. Both of the Members have other jobs outside the Company, as stated in Section 4, above, and are expected to spend most of their working time for their outside employment. Nevertheless, in the event a Member is unable to devote sufficient time to his/her responsibilities as set forth in Section F, above, to the extent that it adversely impacts the performance of the Company and its business, that Member may be subject to having his/her compensation adjusted, or other measures taken as the Members may mutually agree, notwithstanding any provisions to the contrary contained in Section I, pertaining to equal compensation of Members.
33. As stated above, the Company adheres to the highest standards of personal integrity. Accordingly, all Members shall scrupulously avoid at all times any

activity that could be detrimental to the welfare of the Company and its business. Any such conflict of interest that may arise would be grounds for severe disciplinary measures being taken against the offending Member, up to and including having his/her Membership in the Company revoked or terminated.

J. Buy-Sell Agreement

34. In the event of the death of a Member, the value of the deceased Member's interest in the Company, as determined according to the provisions of Section 37, below, shall be paid to the personal representative of the Member's estate.
35. The value of a Members interest in the Company shall be based on the Book Value of such interest, as determined by the accountant who prepares regular financial statements for the Company.
36. If a Member leaves the Company, his/her employment with the company shall be terminated. The departed Member shall be paid the value of his/her interest in the Company as provided in Section 37, above, except as provided in Section 39, below.
37. If a Member leaves the Company to work for any competitor of the Company, the value of his/her interest in the Company, which shall be paid to the departing Member shall be reduced as the remaining Members may mutually agree.
38. No Member shall sell his/her interest in the Company to any person who is not a Member, unless the interest is first offered for sale to the remaining Members, who have a right of first refusal. Such offer must be in writing. Only if the remaining Members decline to purchase the Member's interest within 30 days of the date of the written offer of sale, may the Member's interest be sold to an outsider who is not already a Member. Any attempt to sell a Member's interest in

violation of the terms of this section J. shall be null and void and will not be honored by the Company.

39. Members shall not be required to sign a Non-Competition agreement, but they shall also observe the above-stated standards of personal integrity and shall take no action that would be detrimental to the Company.
40. Any Member who fails to comply with all the provisions of this Agreement shall have his/her Membership revoked by the other Members.
41. Any offer to buy the Company or its business shall be referred to the Members for evaluation. The Members must agree unanimously in order to sell the Company or its business.

K. Company Dissolution

42. Upon dissolution of the Company, its assets will be offered for sale at their Book Value, first, to the Members in proportion to their respective shares in the Company, and then to the public. Shared assets shall be offered for sale to the public.
43. Any intellectual property owned by the Company, and proprietary information, such as customer lists, and Company files and records shall be disposed of as the Members may mutually agree.
44. The continuing use of the Company name and logo shall be determined by the mutual consent of the members.
45. In the event of a dispute between the Members that cannot be reconciled, the members agree not to resort to litigation in court, but in lieu thereof agree to submit the dispute to binding arbitration under the rules of the American Arbitration Association.
46. This Agreement may be amended only by the unanimous consent of the members.

WITNESS the due execution of this Operating Agreement, consisting of 48 numbered sections on six pages, as of the day and year first written above, by the undersigned Members, being all the Members of XYZ Enterprises, LLC.

________________________ ________________________

XXX, Member XXX, Member

BIBLIOGRAPHY

Works Cited

Bureau, U. C. (2019, Febrary 21). 1947, and 1952 to 2002 March Current Population Survey,2003 to 2018 Annual Social and Economic Supplement to the Current Population Survey. Washington DC.

Hudson, M. (2017, December 1). Retrieved from Forbes: https://www.forbes.com/sites/mariannehudson/2017/12/01/in-depth-angel-investor-survey-sheds-light-on-angel-success/#3c6c480f7d35

Reuters. (2013, March 28). Retrieved from https://www.reuters.com/article/us-usa-stocks-sp-timeline/timeline-key-dates-and-milestones-in-the-sp-500s-history-idUSBRE92R11Z20130328

Trends, S. B. (n.d.). Retrieved from https://www.embroker.com/blog/startup-statistics

Walker, J. E. (2009). *The history of black business in America: Capitalism, race, entrepreneurship.* UNC Press Books.

ABOUT THE AUTHOR

Dr. Shanté P. Williams is a Venture Capitalist, Inventor, Intellectual Property Strategist, Innovation Enthusiast, and Private Investor.

She is the Founder and Managing Partner of RW Capital Partners, an investment firm specializing in commercial real estate and technology development, as well as the Chief Investment Officer for two venture capital funds, Black Pearl Global Investments and Co-Active Capital, managing collectively $50M in funding.

As a Scientist, Dr. Williams helped to discover innovative chemotherapy treatments for high-grade invasive brain tumors.

She turned that scientific knowledge into a fast-rising career in corporate America, becoming the Vice President of Technology Acquisition in the Healthcare sector, the Director of Mergers and Acquisitions in the Consumer Healthcare Industry, and finally, the Director of Intellectual Property in the Electric Drive Vehicle Industry.

As the head of RW Capital, Dr. Williams is committed to ensuring that investors make sound investments in innovating ventures. She uses her technical skills and financial background to help entrepreneurs gain access to capital, combat gentrification, build generational wealth, and become an integral part of the digital economy.

To date, Dr. Williams has helped to build more than three dozen businesses and provides working capital to businesses across the United States.

In the venture capital sector, Dr. Williams continues to break barriers with Black Pearl's fund focused on reducing health disparities across the globe. Black Pearl is an advocate for those that continue to experience inferior outcomes and reduced access.

Co-Active Capital will put much-needed capital into the businesses of under-represented founders.

Dr. Williams is a proud graduate of Winston-Salem State University (BS, Chemistry), The Ohio State University (PhD, in Integrated Biomedical Science specializing in Neuro-Oncology and Pharmacology), and Queen's University of Charlotte (MBA).

Dr. Williams has received numerous awards for her business and entrepreneurship efforts including 2021 Career Mastered Leader in Action, 2020, Opportunity Champion, 2019 Charlotte 50 Most Influential Women recognition, 2018 Athena International Young Professional Award, 2017 Alumni Achiever Award- Winston Salem State University, 2017 Charlotte Chamber Young Professional Entrepreneur Award Winner, and 2017 Charlotte Business Journal 40 under 40 Award.

Dr. Williams also serves the Charlotte Community as Chairman of the Board of Directors for the Charlotte Mecklenburg Black Chamber of Commerce, and former Board Chair Heal Charlotte, a non-profit dedicated to holistic community change.

Made in the USA
Monee, IL
12 July 2021

f956ecc7-f4a8-40d4-bfad-466a61e74317R02